Head Starts
Felt Hats and Headwear

Ewa Kuniczak

Kuniczak (signature)

© **March 2005 Ewa Kuniczak**

First edition March 2005
Reprinted 16 March 2011

ISBN: 0 – 9541143 - 6 - 1

> Printed and published by
> **Felt Head to Toe**
> 23 Glebe Road, Kincardine-on-Forth,
> Alloa, Clackmannanshire, FK10 4QB
> Scotland
> Tel/Fax: 01259-730779
> E-mail: ewa@ feltheadtotoe.co.uk
> Website: http://www.feltheadtotoe.co.uk

Head Starts: Felt Hats and Headwear

© March, 2005 by Ewa Kuniczak

Felt Head to Toe
23 Glebe Road
Kincardine-on-Forth
Alloa
Clackmannanshire
FK10 4QB Scotland
Website: http://www.feltheadtotoe.co.uk

Printed in Scotland

No part of this product may be reproduced in any form, unless otherwise stated, in which case reproduction is limited to the use of the purchaser. The written instructions, photographs, designs projects and patterns, are intended for the personal, non-commercial use of the retail purchaser and are under copyright laws; they are not to be reproduced by any electronic, mechanical, or other means, including informational storage or retrieval systems, for commercial use. Permission is granted to photocopy patterns for the personal use of the retail purchaser.

ISBN: 0 – 9541143 – 6 – 1

Other publications by Ewa Kuniczak
'Felt in the Kitchen' ISBN: 0 – 9541143 –0 –2 © June 2001
'More Felt in the Kitchen' ISBN: 0 – 9541143 -1 – 0 © January 2002
'Yet More Felt in the Kitchen' ISBN: 0-9541143-2-9 © September 2002
'Felt out of the Kitchen' ISBN: 0-9541143-4-5 © October 2003
'Felt Figures Great and Small' ISBN: 0-9541143-3-7 © March 2004
'Sensory Deceptions for Felts and Fabrics' ISBN: 0-9541143-5-3 © July 2004

●●

MISSION STATEMENT

It is my intention to provide quality products and service to inspire creativity and enrich the lives of others, so that they may better understand and develop their skills.

●●

> **Dedication**
> To my grand-daughter Hazel, and all present and future 'Mad' Hatters!

Please note

It is important to remember that this publication has been printed on an Inkjet printer, and therefore every effort must be made to prevent it from becoming wet. When printed pages become wet, the inks will run. For this reason, I have included laminated Prompt Sheets at the back of the book, for your use while wet felting.

No responsibility will be taken for any damage to your printed pages if you disregard this warning.

> **Acknowledgements**
>
> To my Exhibition Workshop Organisers, and all of my marvellously talented students throughout the World, who continue to provide me with many fun-filled and challenging moments. Thank you for encouraging me to progress further towards exploring the potential of ideas and techniques, and to take on even greater challenges! Without you all, I would sit around and just have beautiful thoughts!

Apologies for not mentioning by name some of the students whose work may be featured in this publication, but time has played tricks on my memory. If you recognise your work, please let me know so that I can acknowledge your contribution in future issues. Thank you for being so understanding.

Contents

Introduction . 1

Part One : Hat Fundamentals

Preparation . 3
Equipment . 3
Materials . 4
Exploring a theme . 5

Seamless Felting Method . 7
How to design and make a 'Resist' template . 7
Developments from the basics . 8
A word about Hat Blocks . 9
Preparation of the work area . 10
Preparation of design and layers for felting . 11
Felting method . 12
Blocking and finishing touches . 15
Changing Appearances through Dyeing . 16
Painterly Surface Effects . 16
Varying designs from a single 'Resist' shape . 17
Manipulating Brims . 17
Variations on a 'Cloche' shape . 17
Variations on a 'Bell' shape . 18
Hats with pleats and Folds . 18
New Hats from Old . 18

Multi-form Seamless Felting Method . 19
Preparations for Complex Forms . 19
Felting Method . 19
Blocking and finishing . 22

Berets . 23
Preparation . 23
Considerations for basic beret forms . 23
Developments from the basic form . 25
Felting method for complex berets. 26
Shaping and finishing . 27

Part Two: Alternative Head Wear

Mixed Media Fascinators. 29
Preparation . 29
Felting wire . 29
Assembling the parts . 31

Felt Flower Head Pieces. 33
Simple flower form method . 33
Double flower form method . 37
Shaping and Finishing . 41

Headwear as Sculpture . 43
Advanced Felted Wire method . 43
Felted Mesh method . 45

Gallery . 49

Technical Tips . 51
'Pre-felts' . 51
'Pointillist' Effects . 51
Felt Stiffener . 51
Painterly Effects for Hats . 52
Brims . 52
Substitutes for Ridged Mats . 53
Attaching 'Brim Reed'/Millinery wire . 53
Attaching Petersham Ribbon . 53

In Conclusion . 54

Glossary . 55 .

Illustrations . 57

Resources . 61
Suppliers . 61
Literature . 63
Websites . 63
Useful contacts. 63
Future books . 64

About the Author . 65

Introduction

Throughout the history of mankind, hats and headwear have played an important role in dress code. From earliest times, they have denoted status in Society, as an indication of an individual's standing in the community – whether shaman, tribal chief, warrior; or as contemporary parallels – bishop, Lord Mayor, King, or General. Although nowadays these symbols of status are only worn at ceremonial functions, hats and headwear fulfil wider uses.

One of the primary functions of headwear, is that of providing protection for the wearer against the elements, and felt in particular has fulfilled this admirably for human beings, whether humble or noble. Excavations in the frozen tombs of the Scythians in the Altai mountain regions of southern Siberia/Northern Mongolia, revealed many examples of hoods and head ornaments, dating to approximately 700BC. These can be seen in the Hermitage Museum collection, St. Petersburg. Here can be seen simple sewn felt hoods with ear-flaps to ornate silver-mounted felt plumes, as worn by the 'Ice Princess', who was much publicised on her discovery in recent years. Whatever their significance and function, it is evidence that it was customary for people by then to wear some form of head covering on occasions. This has further been supported by the artefacts from 2600BC, preserved by the arid conditions of the desert in the Ürümchi region in North Western China, that were found with the mummies, which were discovered in the latter part of the C20th.

As felt is an excellent insulator, it is ideally suited for creating protection for the head. It shields the wearer from icy winds, and to a certain extent is water-repellent. Perfect. Not only that, there is further evidence that with the onset of mining and industrialisation, felt was used in the making of helmets worn by tin-miners in Cornwall. These were reinforced with clay and pitch to provide protection for the miners against the rock face of the tunnels where they worked. Furthermore, until recently UK policemen's helmets were reinforced with a layer of felt. Improved technology has made this practice unnecessary, as now these are made from new toughened lightweight material.

With the advent of the popularity of hairdressing and the de-formalisation of dress codes in modern society, the wearing of hats has lost its traditional role and its place in everyday wear. Nevertheless, it has survived, and can now be seen again as growing in popularity, as milliners and artists alike reinvent their skills to adjust to modern tastes and demands. No longer is the approach to hats seen as fulfilling merely function and convention, but has become more concerned with sculptural notions. New materials are discovered and developed into entirely unique forms, so that no longer is there are recognisable overall style. Each milliner has now the capacity to not only create their own individual style, but also to explore their own individual approaches to their work.

This is where the felter has a distinct advantage over the milliner, because they are not limited to working with manufactured materials. Felters can make their own, and not only that, they can colour and sculpt the felt according to the demands of their design. In so doing, it gives them full scope, and enables them to have complete freedom of expression in 3-D terms, while still creating an item that not only complements the wearer, but fulfils the required function of a head covering, or adornment.

Introduction

It is with this in mind that I have set out to gather the information together, so that anyone who wishes can not only undertake hatmaking projects in their own way, but can do so with the confidence that the methods described will help them achieve this without sweat or tears. My aim is to help develop sound working practices that produce quality results, and above all, that they promote originality.

I firmly recommend that if you are a beginner that you start modestly with a simple design, so that you can master the techniques, and then progress to more ambitious projects. Once you have mastered the working methods, and have proved to yourself that you can do so to your own satisfaction, you can move on to the next stage with greater confidence. Whatever you do, keep an open mind while you work, and allow yourself to follow directions suggested by the felt when it is made. Exciting and unexpected results can often occur when you allow yourself to work intuitively. There is no such condition as 'failure'; it is merely an attitude of mind! Look upon the 'unexpected' as a design opportunity, and if all else fails, don't be afraid to cut into your felt and play with the results. Over the years, I have rescued many a 'disaster' as seen by my students, and turned it into a masterpiece. Allow yourself to develop 'magic fingers' by keeping your mind open to regarding your finished felt with fresh eyes. Save your original idea for another day, and just go along with the way the felt evolves in your hands!

Above all, enjoy each experience, and as you progress you will be amazed at how inventive you can become. Believe me, you are always learning something new, and I never cease to be astonished by the possibilities, which is why my mind is perpetually coming up with new notions and my enthusiasm never dies!

Part One
Hat Fundamentals

Preparation

The first thing, that needs to be done, is to assemble all the equipment and materials that you may need for your felting project. This need not be expensive, as when you start looking around, you probably will find that much of what you need is already in your home, garage, loft, or dark forgotten corner. Before you buy anything, ask your friends and neighbours if they have any of the items you are seeking. You will be surprised what 'gems' are uncovered in this way. However, you may find that a 'spinner' (not a to be confused with a 'spin-drier') is a useful addition. It saves on drying time, and also helps remove excess moisture from used towels when you have finished the felting. I would be lost without mine, but it is not essential because you can remove surplus moisture from the felts by wringing them out in dry towels.

Another useful piece of equipment is a large metal, or plastic, tray, which is placed on the table to save the number of towels that you use in order to soak up the excess water while you are felting. If some holes are drilled in one corner, the water can drain away into a bucket or basin, placed on the floor beneath. For years I used a large plastic tray that had been found in a skip, until I visited Norway where I was able to buy an even larger galvanised metal tray that had been purpose-built. Magic!

Equipment

- Old towels
- 2 x Nylon net curtains, or Mosquito window mesh, or plastic non-slip matting, cut slightly larger than intended project
- 1 x piece Bubble wrap
- 2 x Plastic Sheeting, cut slightly larger than the project
- Cane window blind with fitting removed
- Approx. 2" (5cm) dia. Piping (width of blind) – foam pipe-insulation lagging is a cheap alternative
- Approx. 1" (2cm) dia. Piping (or wooden dowelling) (width of blind)
- Pipe with ridges (Not essential, but useful)
- Glycerine soap (or other low lather)
- Pieces of glycerine soap for making soap solution (or Norwegian liquid 'Green' Soap)
- Sprinkle bottle (old plastic milk bottle with holes drilled in screw top)
- Wash board, or some kind of board with ridges
- Small plastic bowl and jug
- Distilled Vinegar
- Various plastic basins and bowls
- Scissors and tape measure
- Small plastic mat with ridges [Table mat (a) from IKEA] is useful for making cords, tassels, and flowers
- Iron and ironing board
- Hat Block
- Meat tenderiser for hat brims
- Knicker elastic (for hats only)
- Plastic templates for 'resists'
- Plastic vegetable bag, cut open
- Small trolley with wheels by your workspace is useful (b)

Examples of alternative Hat Blocks and vegetable nettings

Preparation

Comparison of a block made by turning a piece of wood on a lathe and varnished (left), and a standard commercially produced one (right): Both are equally good, though as the commercial one is oval it gives a better fit to a head. I will go into greater detail on this topic in future chapters. It is worth noting though that not all heads are oval, as it is a characteristic of Asians for theirs' to be round. You can find all sorts of alternatives to hat blocks, e.g. bowls, saucepans, and even flowerpots and gourds! Take your tape measure and start searching to find what will fit your head.

The best vegetable nettings are those usually found holding large quantities of onions, Brussels sprouts and turnips. Cut open and machine stitched to stop fraying, and they are perfect for all projects.

Materials for wet felting

Commercially combed Merino 64's wool 'Tops' are recommended for fine quality wet felting. Gotland and Falkland wools can also produce a good quality felt. Both felt easily, but I find Merino gives me the finest results and is by far the easiest to work with. It is my preferred wool type, and one that I use invariably when I am wet felting. I have also discovered that the 'Tops' I have dyed myself will not only give me a more subtle, painterly effect, but will felt more easily and quickly than the commercially dyed ones.

It is therefore worth spending some time before you start your project, dyeing up the colours that you need. In this way not only will you end up with the colours that you require, but also a whole range of related colours that you had not expected. Surprise! What a joy, to have such a rich palette at your fingertips!

The dyes suitable for colouring wool 'Tops', and all other 'protein' (Animal) fibres, are **Acid Dyes**. There are many from which to choose, but I favour **Omega All-in-One Dyes**, as they are very easy to use and produce good results. As you do not have to add any acetic acid (Vinegar), they are relatively non-toxic. However it is recommended that you work in a well-ventilated room, and wear a mask, whenever you are dyeing. I do my dyeing outdoors in the garden on a fine day, which is much more pleasant and it does not fill the house with the smells of wet wool! That way it keeps everyone happy.

Having assembled the equipment you need and gathered together the colours you are going to use, the next thing to consider is the **inspiration** for your hat……………..

Exploring a Theme

True originality does not miraculously appear out of thin air! It has to be fed, nurtured, and stimulated by personal experience. There is nothing more potent than that! Observe, consider, select, and assimilate.

How do you do that? Choose a subject, or theme that really interests you, and ask yourself, "Why?" What qualities excite me?

Can't decide? Start collecting visual reference material – books, pictures, take photographs and make sketches from personal observation whenever possible. All of these will help you select, and identify qualities that most impress you. You may not use all of your ideas, so put them aside for another day! I have many favourite themes that I return to repeatedly, and each time I rediscover them by looking through my collections, and become excited once again. Every time you review your research, you will do so with fresh eyes, and draw renewed inspiration from it.

To illustrate this point, I will show you how ideas can evolve from a visit to a local Sea Life Centre.

As the Centre was crowded with visitors, I took as many photographs on this occasion as I could. When I returned home, I began looking through my books for added inspiration, and began to simplify shapes and cut them out of newspaper.

In this way I was gradually becoming aware of the potential for using them in various seamless projects – bags and cushions – as well as a wealth of Hats and Headwear! Seamless felting where templates are used, rely on well-defined shape as their basis. This will become more apparent when the method is described in the next chapter.

Exploring a Theme

The shapes of angel fish, colours, spikes and tentacles from sea anemones, corals – all made an impression on me. One idea led to another, and before long I had a whole collection of related hats, headwear, and even bags, that I never could have imagined had I not taken the trouble to examine subjects at first hand.

And so the ideas keep coming – in a never-ending progression. The theme is far from exhausted, but at least this gives you an idea of what is possible if you allow yourself to explore the notion of 'hats and headwear' from a different perspective. Consider 'Form' first before 'Function', and allow yourself to investigate ideas for their own sake. I firmly believe that in this way you will discover new and unique concepts that are different from the norm. Once you have the ideas, then you can apply them to a practical solution…………………..

Seamless Felting Method

Before you can start making a hat, you must first prepare your 'Resist' template, around which you will build up the layers for the seamless felt.

How to design and make a 'Resist' for seamless hats? This method can also be applied to other projects. Choose a thick, but pliable plastic, e.g. vinyl, builders' damp-proofing membrane, plastic shelf lining, carpet 'treads' (used for protecting a carpet, especially in hall entrances), or underlay for laminate flooring. If you are going to create a design that is symmetrically arranged on the surface, it is advisable to use a transparent plastic for your 'Resist', because then you can see exactly where your design is placed on the underneath side, when you turn your work over to continue laying out your design on the topmost side.

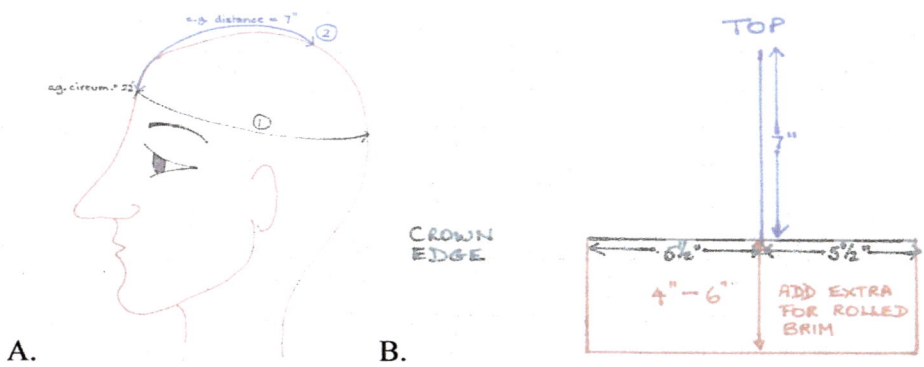

A.   B.

- Measure round your head (1) as shown in diagram A, e.g. 22". This is called the 'crown' for the purposes of these instructions. Next, measure from just above the eyebrows to the centre of your head at the back (2), e.g. 7". You can usually feel a little dent there.
- On a large piece of paper (diagram 'B'), draw a line representing the crown edge, but halve the original measurement of your crown, e.g. 22" will become 11" marked on the line. Find the centre, and draw a vertical line as (2) measurement, e.g. 7".
- Decide on the amount of turn up, or roll that you intend for your finished hat brim, and add that below your crown edge line, e.g. 4" – 6".
- Join up all you points and curve the sides towards the top, as in diagram. This should give you an outline of a basic 'cloche' shape. This now represents the finished size you are aiming at with your felt. (c)

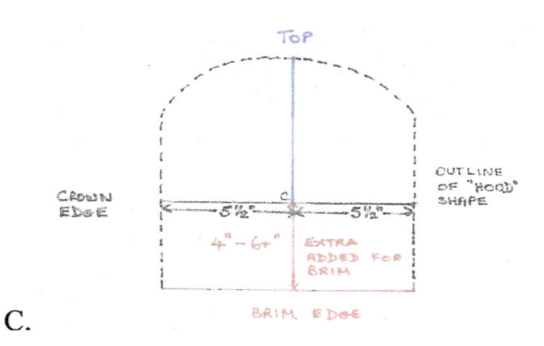

C.

Seamless Felting Method

❏ Before you cut out your resist, you must make allowances for shrinkage, and you do this by adding approximately 2" on all outside edges, as shown at the top of the diagrams below.

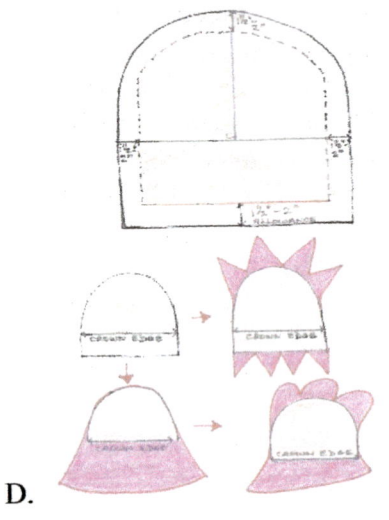

D.

❏ If you want to create different shapes for your hat resists, or add a brim that will form a wide brim finish, you can add extra areas, as indicated by the shaded pink colouring. To be on the safe side exaggerate these shapings, because they very often flatten out to a certain extent during the felting.
❏ Now you are ready to cut out your plastic 'resist' template. Cut out the paper pattern you have just made. Draw round it on the plastic, and cut it out.
❏ You are ready to start making your hat, and of course in future you can design any shape that takes your fancy! You are in control, and the future looks exciting.

However, before I explain the basic felting preparation and method, we need to examine the various types of hat blocks that are so essential to the design and final shaping of your hat.

Seamless Felting Method

A word about Hat Blocks

There are many different types of hat block available for sale, and few of us have the means to buy every kind that you may possibly need for your hat projects. They are expensive to buy new, but it is possible to find used ones in antique shops and car-boot sales. I have even seen them used as doorstops in restaurants! If you are going to invest in good quality wooden ones, choose a dome-topped one and a flat-topped one to begin with, because with those you can shape most forms, including 'pill-box' styles. A useful addition to your collection would be a hat-stretcher, as then you are able to make hats to all sizes.

(clockwise from top left) examples of variously shaped commercial hat blocks, 'blocks' made on a lathe with laminated wood and varnished, lightweight polystyrene ones, and circular lathe-turned 'blocks' with domed tops.

(Left and centre) Example of a top hat 'knock' block; (right) A Hat Stretcher, which can be extremely useful if you only have a few blocks in a limited number of sizes. You use it by placing the finished hat while it is still damp, on it, and turning the large screw on the side, until it reaches the desired size. Leave to dry.

I have found that although I have a large collection of hat blocks now, I actually use only a few basic ones on which I model and manipulate the felt for my hats, using nothing more than my hands, hot iron, and a rolled up towel!

Seamless Felting Method

Furthermore, for brimmed hats, it is not essential to have use of a brim block. Once again, I improvise with a rolled up towel, and a hot iron, while occasionally I have also made a brim block by taping together a piece of foam pipe insulator to form a circle. This I place inside the brim (between crown and brim) and press into shape with a hot iron while the felt is still damp.

Now that you have gathered together all your equipment, materials, and made your 'Resist' template, you are ready to commence preparing and making the seamless felt for your felt hat.

Preparation of the work area

* Prepare your table, by placing a towel on it
* Place the cane mat on top
* Make up a warm soap solution, by dissolving some glycerine soap in warm water, and fill the 'sprinkle' bottle. Remember that when this solution becomes cold while you are working, you can transfer the liquid into a microwave jug, and heat it up for about 2 minutes in the microwave.
* If you have a large tray to work in, place that on top. Otherwise, place a piece of plastic on top of the cane mat

Once you have done that, you are ready to begin building up the design and layers wool for your hat…………………..

Seamless Felting Method

Preparation of Design and Layers for Felting

It is essential before you commence, that you check the 'Resist' template you have made, and that it is large enough to allow for shrinkage during the felting. Otherwise, you will end up with a child's hat instead of one for yourself! Remember that Merino wool shrinks to about 1/3 rd to ½ of its original size.

What you do

1. Place a piece of plastic sheet in the tray, or on the cane blind.
2. Sprinkle the 'Resist' template with soap solution, and rub extra soap all over both sides. This will ensure that anything you place on the surface will stay exactly where you put it. In this way you can control the design build-up, without the fear that anything will move, while you work.
3. **REMEMBER whatever you place down first on to the surface of the 'Resist' template, will show uppermost when the felt is turned right side out. Whatever is nearest the plastic 'Resist', is going to be the OUTSIDE layer of the hat, when it is finished.** Working right side inwards, in this manner, gives maximum protection to that all important outside layer of the hat. In the early stages of felting there is a great deal of friction and movement on the layer nearest the roller, and thus this 'lining' layer could result in some degree of distortion. Whatever is on the inside, nearest the plastic 'Resist' felts gently, and is therefore protected.
4. **On side 'A' of the 'Resist'**, place any shapes cut from 'pre-felts' * (See 'Technical Tips'), and layer any painterly colours where you need them. Sprinkle with soap solution. Cover with a plastic sheet, and turn over to side 'B'.
5. **Remover plastic sheet from side 'B'**, bring any surplus wool over the edges on to side 'B', and complete laying out the design. Sprinkle with soap solution. Cover with plastic, and flip back to side 'A'.
6. **Remove plastic sheet from side 'A'**, and commence laying down the first layer of coloured wool. When complete, sprinkle with soap solution. Cover with the plastic sheet, and turn over to side 'B'.
7. **Remove plastic sheet from side 'B'**, and bring up any surplus wool around the edges, so that they lie on top. Complete the first layer of coloured wool, following the colouring of side 'A', seen through the plastic. Sprinkle with soap solution, and cover with a plastic sheet. Flip over back on to side 'A'.

Seamless Felting Method

8. **Continue building up the next layer on sides 'A' and 'B'** as in steps (6) and (7), but lay the wool in the opposite direction, i.e. at 90° to the first layer. Use a colour that will blend with the colouring of the first layer. 
9. **Layer 3** is laid down in the same direction as Layer 1, using a colour that will blend with the lining colours that you are going to use. Follow the procedure for steps (6) and (7).
10. **Layer 4** is laid in the opposite direction, as for layer 2, using the colours that will show on the underneathside of the hat, and when the brim is turned up. Follow the procedure for steps (6) and (7). 
11. **Surface colouring** can now be added where necessary – first on side 'A' and then side 'B'. Remember to use the plastic sheet to cover your work before you turn it from one side to the other.
12. **Remove plastic from side 'A', and cover with vegetable netting.** Rub extra soap over the surface, and press down with your hands, working from the outside edges towards the centre. Cover with a net curtain, and flip everything over on to side 'B'.    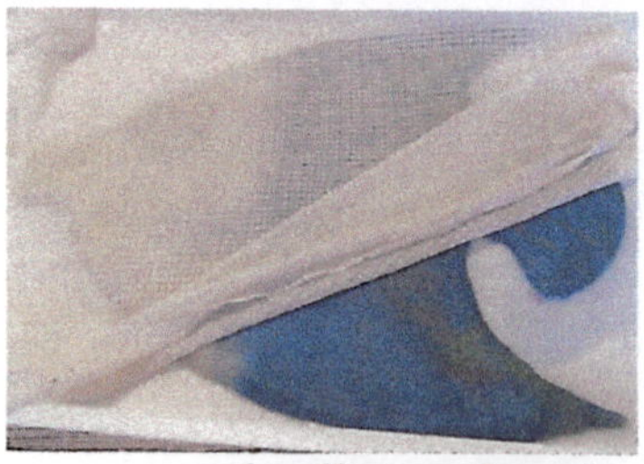
13. **Remove plastic from side 'B', and repeat as in step (12)**

<u>Felting Method</u>

14. **The curtain netting now covers both sides.** Place the work on to the cane mat, and roll up using the larger diameter pipe (roller). 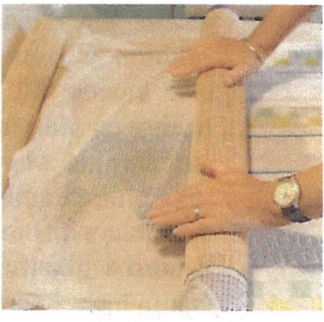 
15. Commence rolling in one direction.
16. Unroll and ¼ turn your work, and commence rolling in the new direction.
17. Repeat this until you have rolled the work in all directions.
18. Turn the work over and repeat rolling, and ¼ turning as in (16) and (17)
19. Repeat this on both sides once more.

Seamless Felting Method

20. **Remove the curtain netting,** and continue rolling, and changing direction on both sides until you notice that the wool has begun to shrink round the 'Resist', and it is actually difficult to roll. 
21. **Place the tray or a plastic sheet back on to the mat.** Cut the hat along the brim edge. 
22. **Remove the 'Resist'.**
23. **Turn Right side out.**

24. **Place the felt on the plastic sheet or tray.**
25. **Cover with the vegetable netting, and sprinkle liberally with VERY HOT soap solution.** (a) Rub extra soap all over, and using the flat of your hand (or a piece of grooved wool) rub the surface backwards and forwards, like a 'sander'. (b)

(a) 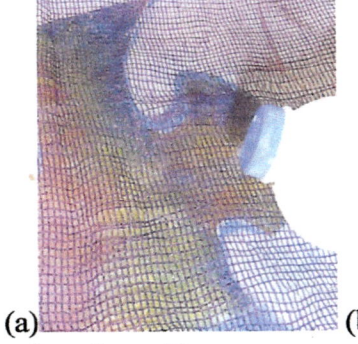   (b)

26. **Repeat on the other side.**
27. **Remove netting, and commence rolling the felt in the mat, using the large roller.** Unroll, and change direction. Roll up and continue rolling in the new direction. Unroll and change direction. Roll up and continue rolling in a new direction. **You will have completed rolling in 3 directions at this stage.** 
28. **Open up the hat, and rub the 'seam' with your hands** to smooth out any ridges that may have formed.
29. **Move the hat round, so that you are not rolling it continually with the fold in the same place.**
30. **Continue rolling in different directions, using the large roller in the mat, making sure you open out the hat and moving it round to prevent any creases forming.** Continue doing this until you have rolled the hat in all directions. By now the felt should be feeling fairly firm.

Seamless Felting Method

31. **Place the hat on the mat so that only the brim edge is in the mat.**
32. **Using the fine dowel rod or pipe, commence rolling the brim in the mat. Press down hard as you do this.** By rolling the brim edge more in this manner, you are making it firmer. Periodically open out the hat, and move it round so that you avoid felting in creases.
33. **When you have working your way round** until you reach the position where you started, move the whole felt into the centre of the cane mat, and continue rolling in all directions, making sure that you open out the hat, and move it round so that avoid folds felting into creases. 
34. **If you have a pipe with ridges, wrap the felt round the pipe and roll on the mat, until you have worked in all directions.** This helps to toughen the felt, while keeping it smooth at the same time.
35. **Place the hat on a washboard, and pour boiling water into it.** This sudden change of temperature will 'shock' the felt, and cause it to shrink further.
36. **Knead the felt on the washboard with your hands.** This action will 'firm' up the felt, and make it denser. This is called, 'Fulling'; a process that is also used in firming up woven cloth.

The felting process is now complete, and can be applied to all basic seamless projects.

Finishing the Felt
1. **Rinse out the soap in plenty of warm water, until the water it clear.**
2. **Place the felt in a 'Vinegar Bath'**, made up of approximately 1 tablespoon of Vinegar to 1 litre (2 pints) Water. This will neutralise the wool, and restore the PH value of the wool. If it contains soap, it will remain alkaline and may cause the fibres to rot in time.
3. **Spin out excess moisture.** If you do not have a spinner, wrap the felt in a dry towel, and place it on the floor. Stamp all over it, and your body weight will press out the excess moisture.

The felt is now ready for the next stage - 'Blocking' the hat. This where the fun begins!

Seamless Felting Method

Blocking the Hat

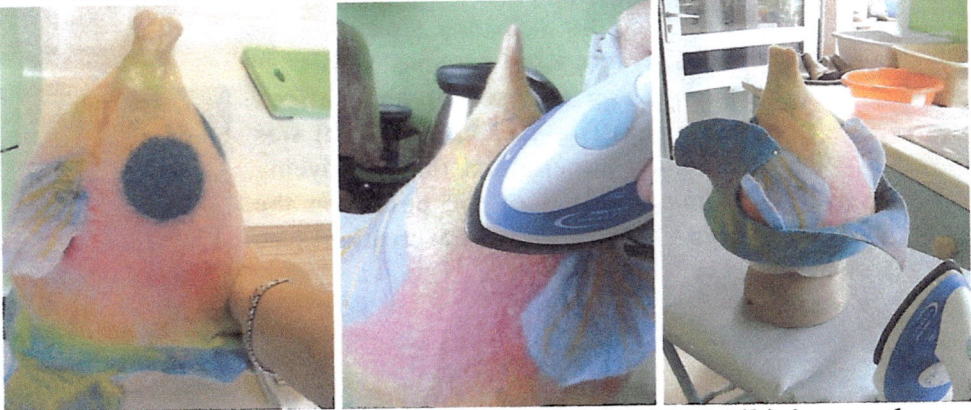

1. Choose a block that is ½" (1.5 cm) larger than your actual head size, for a comfortable fit.
2. Place the felt on the hat block, and pull down firmly all round, keeping your hands on opposite sides of the block, as you do so. This enables you to maintain an even tension.
3. Iron the whole felt without trying to do any shaping, until it is smooth.
4. Tie the knicker elastic tightly where the brim will be turned up. This will hold the hat firmly on the block, and prevent it from sliding upwards when you pull the brim up.
5. Pull the brim up, and continue to iron, but this time as you iron, shape the felt with your fingers, and support the felt where necessary with a rolled up towel underneath, as you achieve the desired effect.
6. Use pins to secure the felt in position, and leave to dry naturally.
7. Remove the pins and elastic, and take the hat off the block.

Finishing Touches

1. Stitch the felt where necessary to maintain the design. I use tiny stitches, worked from the inside of the hat, so that they remain invisible on the outside.
2. For a professional touch, sew in your name label.
3. If the hat is too large, you can make it fit more snugly by stitching a 'petersham' band on the inside (see 'Technical Tips').
4. If you or your client are allergic to wool, it may be necessary to make a silk lining, and sew that in place before stitching in the 'petersham' ribbon.

In all the years that I have been teaching, I have never ceased to be amazed at the diversity and richness of ideas produced by my students. It seems that there is unlimited potential in this method of seamless felting. Follow the guidelines, and you too will surprise yourself by what you can achieve!

Hat Workshop, Missenden Abbey, Bucks. England

Seamless Felting Method

Additional Considerations

Changing the Appearance through Dyeing

If you make a white hat, or even a two-tone hat, you can transform it through 'resist' dyeing techniques. Furthermore, if you make a hat using light colours and have areas in contrasting dark colours, you will find that the dyed colour will only appear on the lighter coloured 'ground'. This technique can be used to great effect. Try it. The 'Hoopoe' hat (see left) was completely transformed through dyeing and manipulation of the points on the crown – a completely new creation! (see right)

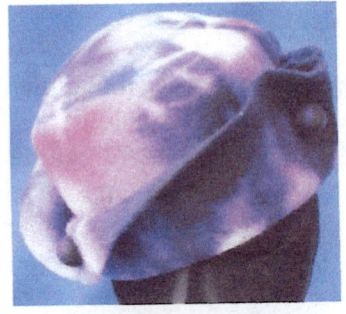

Painterly Surface Effects

Drawing upon the inspiration of works by such artists as Monet (below left and centre) and Seurat (below right), it is possible to create 3-D interpretations in the form of hats. Furthermore, by contrasting the underside of the brim with the top, you are able to create two 3-D paintings in one composition.

Variations on a simple form

Many interesting and stylish designs can be created from the same template by

       a) Cutting into the brim, and twisting or curling the cut edge. See left how the 'Seurat' hat became transformed doing this.
       b) The type and shape of 'block' used for the crown
       c) Various ways in which the brim is manipulated

Seamless Felting Method

How is it possible to vary the design of hats from a single 'resist' shape?
Try cutting at an angle into the brim of the finished hat, after you have 'blocked' it, and ironed it. For this you will need a sharp pair of scissors. Do not be frightened. You will be surprised how many variations you can come up with every time you do this. I have done this many times, and I have never achieved the same result! Do this while the hat is still damp, because you can iron and 'steam' the shapings, adjusting with your fingers until you achieve the effect you desire. Pin in place, and leave to dry. Sew the cut pieces invisibly with a matching thread, and stiffen with a 'felt stiffener'. (See 'Technical Tips' for information on the use of stiffeners) The permutations are limitless!

Manipulating brims
This is done during the 'blocking' of hats, using your fingers, a hot iron, and with the additional support of a folded, or rolled up towel. You can spend as long as you like doing this, until you arrive at a satisfactory solution. As you work, turn the hat round so that you see it from all angles.

Variations on a 'cloche' shape

In the example on the far right, can be seen the dramatic transformation made by incorporating tassels and points on top of the crown, as well as the effect made by 'blocking' on a conical block.

Seamless Felting Method

Variations on a 'bell' shape
This is the usual shape used for wide-brimmed hats, and can be modified in a number of different ways, e.g. by making one side wider than the other. (See p.8, diagram 'D')

Hats with Pleats and Folds
In order to create hats with folds, and additional contouring, you need to plan for this when you are designing the 'Resist' template. Allowances have to be made for the extra felt that will be required for such manipulations. The size and shaping has to be exaggerated to accommodate these types of sculptural effects. Edwina's hat (right) was created using a template that was HUGE, but it did allow plenty of scope for manipulating into shape. Furthermore, it is recommended that as you build up the layers for the felt, that you do so making them much finer than when preparing for just a basic hat form. So, think 'thin' and think 'extra large' where you intend to incorporate pleats. Otherwise, you will find that either you do not have enough felt in the hat for the pleats, or that the hat becomes heavy-looking and lumpy.

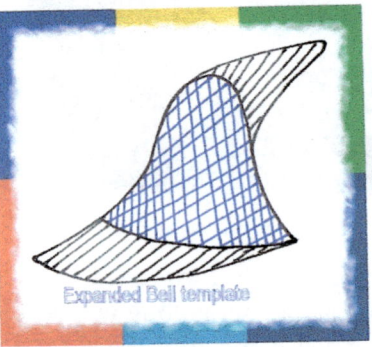

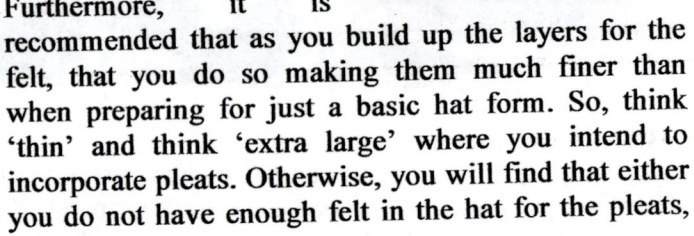

New Hats from Old
There are occasions when you have made a hat and after a while you are either tired of it, or you no longer like it. Re-modelling hats is extremely easy with hand made felt. Soak the hat overnight in warm water. Spin out the surplus moisture, and you are ready to re-block it, cut into it, or do whatever else comes to mind. There are infinite possibilities for reviving old designs, and in this way your hat has extended its life and usefulness.

Multi-form Seamless Felting Method

The actual felting process is the same as in the previous chapter (Seamless Felting Method), but the preparation is entirely different. What is the advantage? With this particular method you are not limited to relying on the silhouette type template for your design, as in the previous chapter. You can create any 3-D form, because you can accommodate additional sections that jut outwards in different directions from the foundation silhouette – thus giving you greater freedom.

The preparation for the multi-form seamless method is different to the one described in the previous chapter, where you had to think in reverse, i.e. placing the outer layers of the hat nearest the template, and then building up the layers towards the 'lining'.

With the multi-form method, I have found it is easier to start laying down the lining colours first (nearest the plastic template), and build up to the outer layer and surface design of the hat. In some respects this way of working is easier to understand, but the drawback is that you have to be extra vigilant about creating ridges during the preparations and actual felting process. It is easier to disguise ridges when they occur on the underside of a hat, than on the top surface. This is one main consideration when you decide working in this way. It is therefore not recommended for the complete beginner. I would suggest that you first master the seamless method described in the previous chapter, and then progress to the multi-form version, because it is complicated and fiddly in its preparation. Get the feel of handling the material, controlling the layers, and avoiding a build up of surplus fibres around the edges of the template.

Method
1. Prepare the plastic template as described in the previous chapter, and fix additional plastic shapes to the surface with masking tape. ('Sellotape' is not suitable for this, as it loses its stickiness when it becomes wet.
2. Sprinkle both sides of the template and rub extra soap on all surfaces.
3. Star wrapping the first layer of wool around the extra plastic shapes in turn, making sure that you do not make them too thick.
4. Sprinkle soapy water on each one. Cover with a vegetable net, and rub extra soap on. Press each one in turn between your hands to ensure that each one is thoroughly wetted through, and all fibres are holding together.

Multi-form Seamless Felting Method

5. Repeat this on both sides of the hat template. 
6. Begin to cover the hat template with wool, starting at the top, and working your way down towards the brim edge. As you do this, move the additional covered shapes out of the way, while you place the wool down on to the surface of side A. 
7. Work your way in this manner, changing the colour you use as you near the brim edge because this will show when the brim is turned up, when the hat is complete. 
8. Sprinkle the remainder of wool on side A. Cover with plastic sheet, and turn over to side B. Remove the plastic, and place any surplus wool that is around the template, so that is lies on top of the surface. **It is important to take care that the wool on the edges remains close to the template, otherwise unsightly ridges will form. (i.e. that before laying down the wool for side B, the surplus has been brought over from around the edges, as seen on left.)**  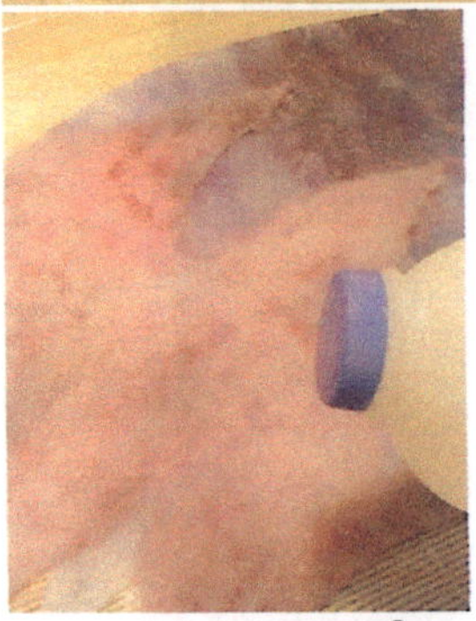
9. Begin to lay down the wool on side B as you did for side A.
10. On completion, sprinkle the surface with warm soapy water. Cover with plastic sheet, and flip over, ready to commence 2nd layer on side A. 
11. **Before laying down the wool for the 2nd layer, make 'tails'**, if you wish to have 'sprouty' bits coming out of the points. * (optional)

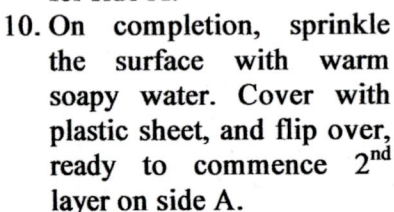

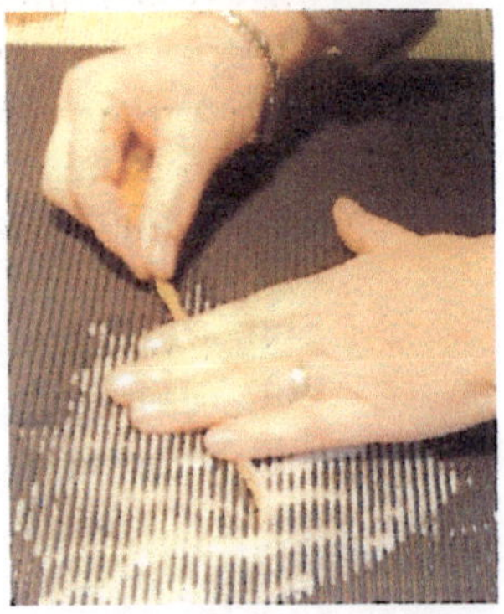

Making 'Tails'
   a) Pull off lengths of 'Tops'. Fold each in half. Hold one end in your hands and keep it dry. Dip into warm soapy water.
   b) Add extra soap to the wet section, and roll on ridged mat until it is firm. Make sure you keep the end in your hands, dry throughout.
   c) Divide the dry end of the each 'tails', and place the wool on each point so that the wool is spread out on both sides of each shape -see i). If you wish to group several 'tails' together, divide them up so that they are not all laying down on the same side – see ii).

Multi-form Seamless Felting Method

i)    ii)

12. **Second Layer:** Lay the wool down in the opposite direction to the 1st layer, using the colour that will show on the outside of the hat. As you build up the layer, sprinkle with warm soapy water to ensure everything will stay in place. 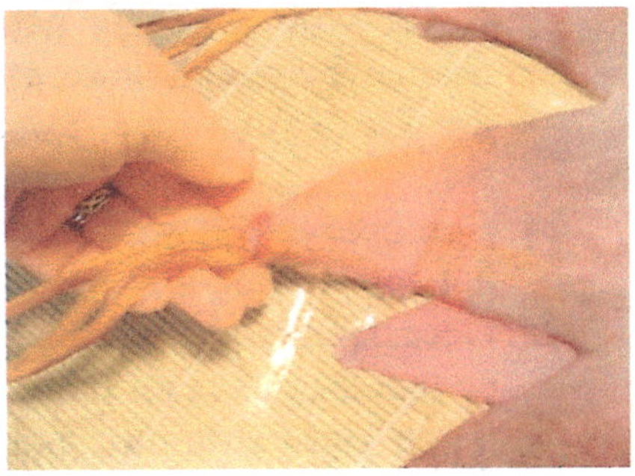 
13. Build up the top layer on the extra shapes as you come to them, in the same manner.
14. Continue building up the layer, on side A until the whole has been completed. Sprinkle with warm soapy water. Cover with a plastic sheet and flip over to side B. 
15. Remove the plastic sheet, and bring the surplus wool over the edges so that it lays on top of the surface of side B.
16. Repeat as for side A (steps 12 –14)
17. Flip over to side A. Remove the plastic sheet, and squeeze the points gently with soapy hands to ensure that there are no ridges. 
18. Cover with a veggie net, and rub extra soap on to the surface. Press with hands from the outside edge of the template towards the middle. This helps to reduce the risk of the wool spreading sideways.
19. Cover with a nylon curtain, and flip over to the other side.
20. Repeat steps 18-19, on this side.
21. Commence rolling with the large roller ¼ turning in the usual way as described in the previous chapter. When you have completed rolling on both sides twice, remove the nylon curtain netting, and continue rolling without it until the plastic template either begins to curl, or it is difficult to roll because the wool has shrunk. 
22. Cut open along the brim edge, and **turn inside out.**

Multi-form Seamless Felting Method

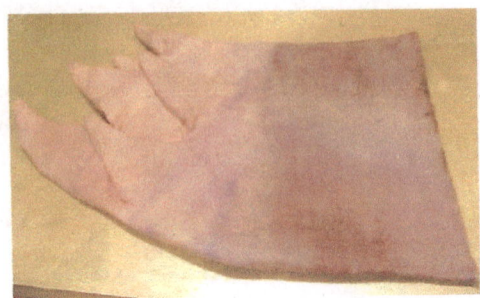

23. Cover with a veggie net. Sprinkle hot soapy water generously all over to change the temperature. Rub extra soap over the surface, and rub all over with the flat of your hand, like a flat-bed sander. Turn over and repeat on the other side.
24. Continue to roll with the large roller ¼ turning on both sides, opening up the hat and moving it round so that you avoid ridges forming on the sides.
25. Occasionally pick up the hat and rub with your hands, shaping the extra points so that they have no ridges.
26. **Turn right side out**, and continue rolling with a smaller roller, and shaping with your hands occasionally, until you create the desired effect.
27. Shock the felt by placing it on a washboard and pouring boiling water into it. Knead it on the board with your hands.
28. Rinse out the soap thoroughly, and pass through a vinegar rinse bath.
29. Spin dry, or roll into a dry towel to remove the surplus moisture.
30. Stretch on to a hat block.

Blocking and Shaping
* Use a rolled up towel to help the shaping.
* As you work, smooth the felt with a hot iron, and pull it into shape.
* Make the tucks and twists as you heat the felt with the iron, securing the shaping with pins as you progress.
* Leave to dry
* When dry secure the shapings in position with small 'invisible' stitches, worked on the inside of the hat.

And voila! It's finished, and ready for the finishing touches of sewing your label on the inside.

Berets

Of all the headwear that you can design and make, probably the simplest would be the Beret. Yes, it is simple in as much as you do not have to 'block' it or worry about brims, but there are a few considerations to which I would like to draw your attention.

- ❖ They need not conform to the conventional shape that you buy in shops. You can make them quite **extra-ordinary,** even though they may conform to the basic circular shape! They could follow a theme. A Pizza is circular. So are many berries – see the pun-like connection with the word, 'berets'? You can have so much fun with those ideas alone!

- ❖ Other inspirations for berets can be insects. Many of them are actually circular in appearance, e.g. ladybirds.

- ❖ **Openings** need not always be a circle cut for the head, in the centre on the underside. In fact you can get some very interesting results by placing them off centre. But why always have circles cut for the head? Why not cut a slit instead? This will alter the way the beret sits on the head. It will make it far more sculptural in appearance. Try it. If you do not like it, you can always cut out a circle afterwards. No problem.

Opening variations

  A. Slit in the centre
  B. Slit off centre
  C. Oval slightly off centre
  D. D Circle off centre

- ❖ Why not try a different shape for the beret? It does not always have to be circular.
    A. Area representing original head size
    B. Additional 2"- 3" (5 - 7cms) added to allow for shrinkage
    C. Additional section to change the shaping of the beret

Developing basics

Berets

❖ The beret (left and right) has been extended in this manner, and includes pieces of loosely woven woollen fabric with additional embroidery for extra texture and interest.

What special considerations are there for making berets?
❖ One thing often becomes overlooked when building up the layers of wool around the plastic resist you are using. Both the top side and underneath side appear exactly alike! Therefore, to avoid the trauma of having to decide which is which when the time comes to cut into it to remove the plastic, this is what you do. After you have completed each underneath layer, place a mark made by a piece of wool, or a 'pre-felt' shape in a contrasting colour. When you cut through to remove the plastic, you will cut that part away, and all will be well.
❖ **How do you design your plastic 'resist'?** You can either draw round the largest circular tray you have in the house, and hope for the best, or you can be a little more accurate. Measure the circumference of your head, and for simplicity, divide by 3 to find the radius. You do not have to be exactly accurate as felt, on completion, will stretch. Thus if your circumference measures 22", the radius of the circle you need to draw will measure approximately 7.3". Drawn a circle using this radius, and the result will represent your head opening, add a further 3"-4" (depending how large you want the finished beret to be.) **Add another 2" all round the edge for shrinkage**, and you have the pattern for your 'resist'. (See page 23) Use it as it is, or change the shape before you start preparing your layers for felting, and follow the stages for the seamless method. Before you know where you are, you will have a beautiful beret!

Claudie when she made her beret made it extra large to allow for additional manipulation of the surface, so that the finished result looked nothing like a conventional one. The template was more oval in shape, and the opening was eccentric.

Berets

More Advanced Developments

* Using a circular template, complete with shrinkage allowances, the shape can be completely altered, with additional sections.

Circle Beret

Altered template with additional sections

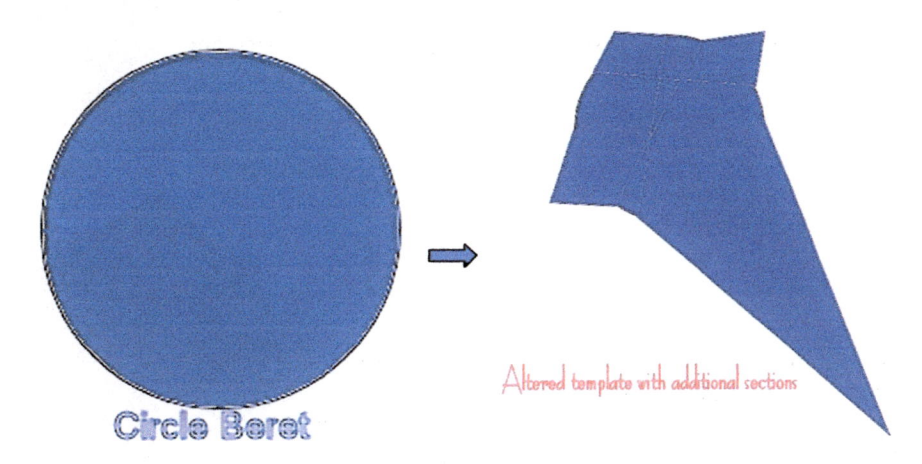

* Further transformations can be created on a circular template by taping additional plastic shapes on to the upper side of the template – thus allowing for additional manipulations. This type of beret is prepared in the same way as the 'Multi-form' seamless method described in the previous chapter.

Additional plastic sections taped to template

Developing a Design for a Beret from a Source

Taking inspiration from a fragment of a shell (a), the template was prepared by taping an additional plastic triangle on to the upper side (b).

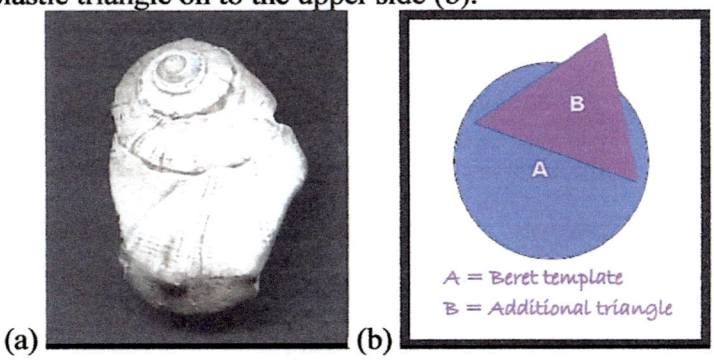

A = Beret template
B = Additional triangle

(a) (b)

Berets

Felting Method for Complex Berets

- ❖ Prepare the layers for the beret, following the method described in the previous chapter, for multi-form seamless felting.
1. Commence by laying down the 1st layer of wool around the triangular section, and then continue to complete the layer on side 'A', making sure that you separate the covered triangular section from the rest of the template layer with a piece of plastic.
2. Sprinkle with soapy water. Cover with a plastic sheet, and turn over to side 'B'. See right.
3. Bring the surplus wool over from around the edges, and lay them on top of the template. Complete the first layer on side 'B'. Sprinkle with soapy water, and cover with a plastic sheet. Flip back over to side 'A'.
4. Bring the surplus wool over from around the edges, and lay them down on top of the wool that that was laid down in step (1).
5. Repeat this on both sides for the 2nd layer, using the colours for the outside of the beret. This will form the outer layer of the beret.
6. (optional) Place a surface pattern on top of this outer layer.
7. Remove plastic from side 'A'. Cover with a vegetable net, and rub extra soap all over. Press down with hands, working from the outside edge towards the centre. As you do so on each area, cover each section with a net curtain, before flipping over to side 'B'.
8. Repeat step (7) on this side, and flip back to side 'A'.  
- ❖ Commence felting by rolling in the mat in all directions, using the large roller, until the wool has shrunk to such an extent that it is difficult to actually roll any more.
- ❖ Cut open, and remove the plastic template. Turn inside out.
1. Cover with vegetable net, and sprinkle generously with **HOT** soapy water to change the temperature. Rub extra soap all over. Turn over to the other side, and repeat.
2. Remove the vegetable net, and commence rolling in all directions with large roller. As you do this, check that the inside is not felting together, by placing your hand inside occasionally and separating the surfaces.
3. Turn right side out, and continue rolling in all directions, using the <u>fine roller</u>.
4. Use your soapy hands to work on the additional section to ensure that no seams have formed. Rub and pull into shape as you work with your hands.

Berets

5. Place on a washboard and pour boiling water into the beret, and knead it on the board in order to make the felt as dense as you can.

❖ Finish off by rinsing out all the soap in plenty of warm water – changing it until the water is clear. Pass through a vinegar rinse, and spin out the surplus moisture.

❖ Place the beret on an ironing board, and press smooth and flat with a hot iron.

❖ Place on a hat block, and begin shaping the spiral, using your fingers and hands continue shaping, using the iron to help you as you work.

❖ Pin the shaping in position, and leave to dry.

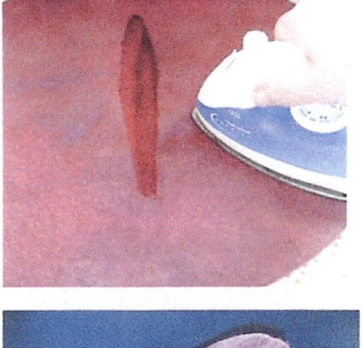

❖ When completely dry, remove the pins, and sew the folds together from the inside to hold them in place.

Another masterpiece completed – and it can be worn in many different ways!

Part Two
Alternative Head Wear

Mixed Media Fascinators

Fascinators can be an imaginative alternative to hats, especially when you have spent a great deal of money having your hair done at the hairdresser's. They can complement your outfit on special occasions, and enhance your appearance. They make you feel special too, and are certainly worth considering as a fashion accessory. In recent years they have gained popularity, and you can give them an individual touch by including handmade felt details.

Once they have been assembled, they can be attached to combs, hair bands, or sewn on to brooch backs and worn as a corsage.

Materials you will need

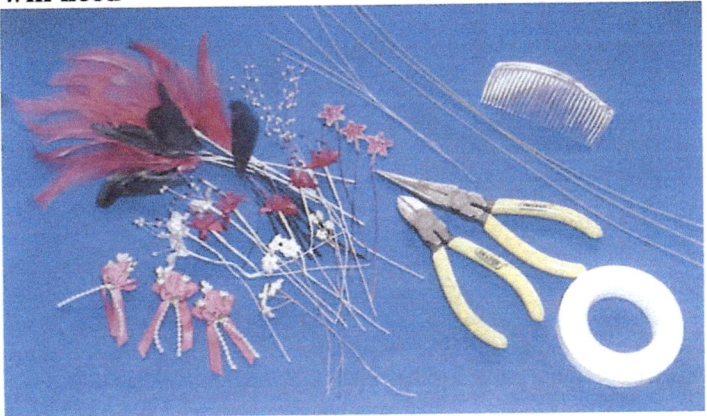

- Cloth covered 18g florist wire for felting
- Dyed Merino 'Tops'
- A selection of feathers, flowers, etc.
- Fine wire for binding pieces together and for fixing the fascinator on to a comb
- Hair comb, hair clasp, or hair band
- Pair of pliers and a pair of wire cutters
- Roll of florist tape

Preparation
Felting the wire
1. Pull off lengths of 'Tops', but make sure they are fine. Thick pieces are difficult to wind on the wire smoothly.
2. Dip a length in a bowl of warm soapy water.
3. Add extra soap to this wetted length, and smooth flat with your fingers.

Mixed Media Fascinators

4. Begin to twist the end of the wool on to the wire, starting about ½ cm from the end of the wire, and wrap towards the tip of the wire.

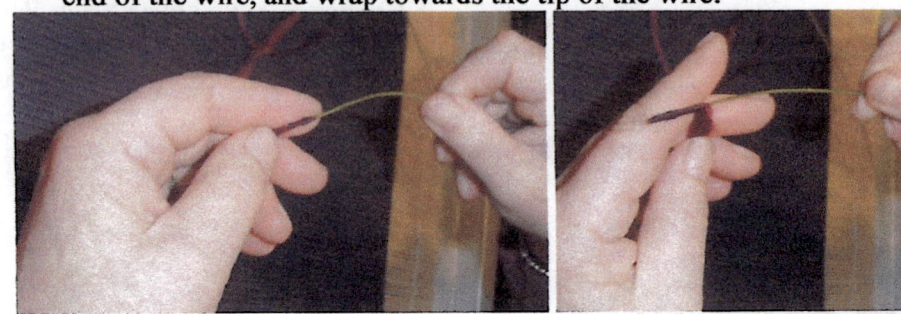

5. When you reach the tip, wrap the wool over this section, and continue wrapping by holding the wool flat against the wire, but turning the wire with your other hand (see above right). In this way you will cover the wire smoothly. When you reach the end of the wire, finish wrapping by covering part of the already wrapped wire so that you do not have any wool ends free at the end of the wire.
6. Dip the wrapped wire in the bowl of soapy water, and rub extra soap along its length. This will help to hold the wool more securely.
7. Roll the wire with your hands on a ridged mat, or cane blind, until the wool has felted together.

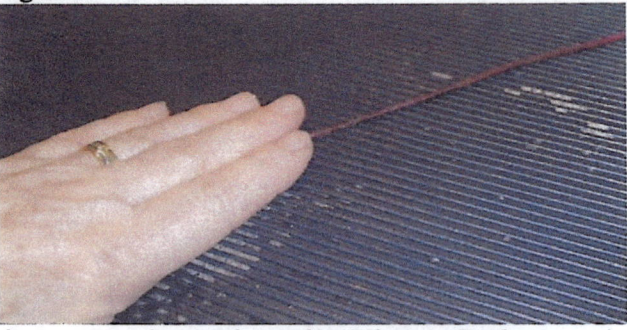

8. Rinse out the soap, and pass through a Vinegar Bath.
9. Roll in a towel to dry.
10. The wires will then be ready to use. Bend each into the desired shapes.

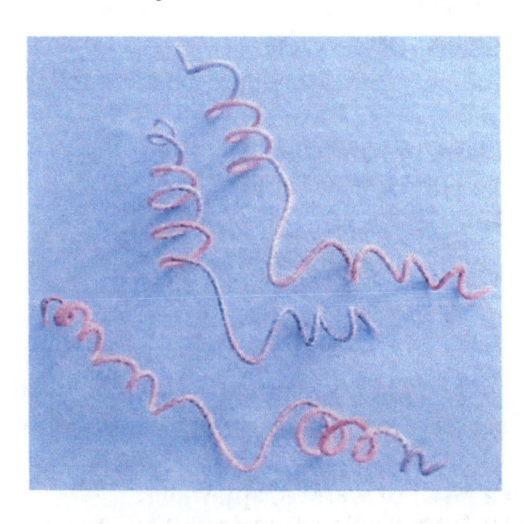

Collect together all the materials you intend to use.

Mixed Media Fascinators

Assembling the parts
1. Begin to twist the feathers and flowers on to the felted wires.
2. Interlock each additional decoration as you build up the design.

3. When you have assembled all the pieces together in this way, cover the tangle of wires with a piece of florist tape. It stretches and sticks together, and makes a perfect seal.
4. Use the fine wire to secure the fascinator on to the comb.

5. Intertwine additional flowers to mask any of the tape that is showing, and cut off any surplus wire with wire cutters.

The fascinator is now complete.

In the next chapters, I will describe how to make decorative felt flowers, which will enable you to make even more elaborate hair decorations.

Mixed Media Fascinators

(Above left and right) Fascinators wired on to hair bands.

(Above left) Orchid Fascinator : (Above right) Titania's Crown

'Swarming Butterflies' headwear and necklace

Felt Flower Head Pieces

The first type of flower I will describe is a single variety, which can be used on its own, or in combination with other elements as suggested in the previous chapter. These flowers can also be used to decorate a wide variety of articles, e.g. hats, bags, and chokers. They are made 'all in one'. No sewing. The only sewing will be at the end when you need to attach them to something. Use Merino 64's 'Tops' for best results.

As everything is so much smaller than any of the other projects discussed so far, you need to scale down the sizes of all your equipment. It is a good idea to have a range of various widths and sizes in the pipes that you use for your work anyway, because you can then select what complements the scale of the project you are undertaking.

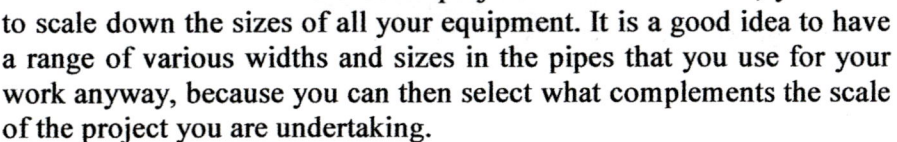

Method

- Essentially the steps are similar to the seamless techniques that I use.
- Before you start, you need to make your 'resist' templates, making allowances for shrinkage. As you are working very small, you need only allow approx. ½" all the way round.

- I prepare and make several at the same time, because when it comes to felting them, it takes as long to felt 5 or 6 as it does to roll one; thus saving time and energy!

    1. The first thing you make are the stamen.
    2. Pull off a small amount of wool from the 'tops', and dip into a bowl of warm soap solution. Soap your fingers, and run them down the length of the piece. Fold the ends in, and wrap a tiny amount of contrasting wool to make a tight 'bead' over the top. Dip in the water, and roll each bead separately in your fingers until they are firmly felted. 
    3. Felt the stamen, but leave about 1" in the middle untouched. You do this by dipping each half in turn into the bowl of soapy water, and rolling them diagonally across the cane blind with the flat of your hand until they are firmly felted. You can make several in this way. Take a tiny amount of green Merino wool and wrap it round the unfelted middle section of the stamen. Wet it gently with your wet soapy fingers to hold the wool in place.

Felt Flower Head Pieces

4. Take a piece of green wool for the stalk, and fold it over the middle of

the stamen.

5. Fold the stem wool in half towards the stamen, and dip into the bowl of warm soapy water. Put extra soap on your fingers, and run them over the stem wool.
6. Felt the stem by rolling diagonally on the cane blind until firm, but be sure to leave the part that is joined on to the stamen under-felted, because this is where the flower will be attached.

Illustration above.

7. Place the flower 'resist' on to a sheet of plastic. Sprinkle with warm soapy water and rub extra soap all over it. Place the stem on the resist, with the stamen on the outside of it, as illustrated. Take a very small amount (cobweb thickness) of coloured wool and lay on the 'resist' to form a painterly effect on both sides, turning the work over in the usual way, using the clear plastic. Place a thin layer of Merino across-ways using the main outside colour for your flower. Wet, and turn over to complete the other side. Turn your work over again, and place a contrasting colour for the inside, laying the wool in the opposite direction. Do this on both sides, wetting each one as you go.

YOU ONLY USE 2 LAYERS for the flowers.

Felt Flower Head Pieces

8. When you have completed all your layers, apply a fine film of contrasting colour as a painterly effect on the surface of your last layer.

9. Cover with vegetable netting, and gently massage extra soap into the surface. Place in nylon curtain netting and roll in the usual manner with pipe and cane blind, removing the netting after you have completed the quarter turns on both sides. Continue rolling in the blind until the 'resist' begins to poke through the corners. Cut open. Cover with vegetable net. Apply hot water with the sprinkle bottle, and rub extra soap on surface. Massage with your hands. Remove the net, and continue rolling until the felt become stable.

10. Place the flower on the edge of the blind, and using your thinnest pipe or dowelling, continue to roll, pressing down hard. Remember to open out the flower and change its position as you work all along its cut edge. Place the flower in the centre of the blind, and roll the whole flower until it is firm.

11. Place on a washboard, and shock with boiling water. Rinse and vinegar rinse. Spin. Pull into shape, and roll the stem in your hands to give it a better shape. Snip in from the edge, and shape your petals. Iron with a hot iron, shaping the petals further with your fingers. Leave to dry.

Felt Flower Head Pieces

You can now apply your flower to hair slides, 'Alice' bands, brooch backs, etc., but first you need to felt these fittings.

Fittings for the flowers

The method for felting these fittings is the same, what ever you choose. Hair slides and brooches are just more awkward, because they are so small.

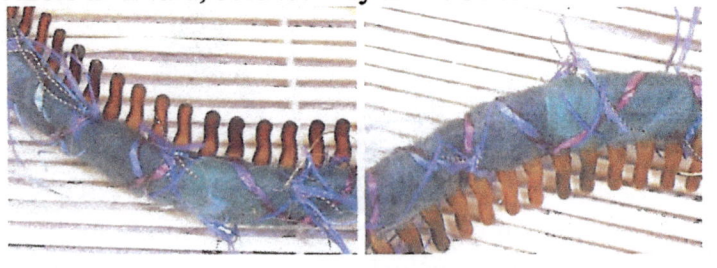

- For slides and brooches, wrap a small amount of wool over the metal bars. Dip in a bowl of warm soapy water, and with soapy fingers rub all over until the wool has felted. 'Alice' bands are easier because they are larger and the 'comb' part grips the wool more easily. They can also be highly decorative if you wrap fancy yarns over the wool before you start felting. These yarns serve another useful purpose in that they hold the wool in place while you rub.
- Once you have wrapped the 'Alice' band with wool and yarn, wet it by dipping all of it into a bowl of warm soapy water. With soapy fingers proceed to rub vigorously over the wool-covered area until it has felted.
- Rinse in warm clear water, and give it a final vinegar rinse, before drying with a towel.
- When your fittings are dry, you can attach your flower, and 'voilá'!

Now you can try your hand at all sorts of other flowers, or even find ways of using them to embellish other creations.

Double Flower Form Method

This is a development from the single flower form method, and once again it is built up in several stages before it is finally felted together.

Many attractive variations can be achieved with this type of flower before further embellishments are added prior to attaching on to a hair comb, slide, or hair band.

It is not the easiest method, as it is fiddly and care must be taken at each stage in order to achieve satisfactory results. If you have mastered making single flowers, this would be a natural progression. Have fun!

Method 
1. Cut 2 templates; 1 smaller one for the inside section; and 1 larger one for the outside section.
2. **Starting with the inside flower section:** Make the stamen and attach the stem, as for the single flower in the previous chapter, and put to one side.
3. Place the small flower template on a piece of vegetable netting on a ridged mat. Moisten with warm soapy water, and rub on both sides with extra soap to make them sticky.
4. Place the stem on to the template, as seen right.
5. Lay down the 1st layer of wool on to the template, and sprinkle with warm soapy water. Cover with a piece of vegetable netting, and turn over on to the other side. Remove the netting.  
6. Bring the surplus wool from around the edges of the template, and smooth them on top of the template.
7. Complete the 1st layer on this side. Sprinkle with warm soapy water. Cover with the veggie netting, and turn over to the first side. Remove the netting. Bring the surplus wool over, as in step 6. See left. 
8. Place the 2nd layer of wool in the opposite direction to the 1st layer. Sprinkle with warm soapy water. Cover with netting, and turn over on the other side.
9. Remove the netting, and complete the 2nd layer on this side, as in step 8.
10. Once the 2nd layer has been completed on both sides, make sure that you have a piece of veggie netting underneath and on top of the covered template.
11. Rub extra soap on both sides (a), and gently squeeze the template in both hands, working your way round in all directions, making sure that you press

Double Flower Form Method

the wool inwards towards the centre (b). This is to make sure that you avoid making ridges on the edges.

(a) (b)

12. Continue by rubbing the surface gently with you hands with the netting in place. See right.
13. Remove the veggie netting, and commence rubbing the surface with your hands, turning your work round as you do so. While you do this, make sure that the wool remains smoothly on the template.

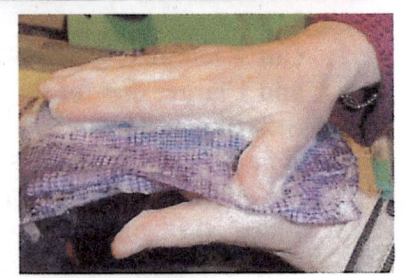

14. Place the template on the cane blind, and begin to roll with a small roller. Continue doing, changing directions frequently, until you notice that the wool is starting to shrink. (The plastic template either begins to curl, or starts poking out of the corners.)

15. Cut along the lower edge, and turn the flower right side out.
16. Place to one side, while you make the 2nd part of the double flower.

Double Flower Form Method

Outside Flower Section 
1. Place a piece of veggie netting on to the ridged plastic mat, and wet and soap the 2nd large template. Place on top and commence laying down the 1st layer.
2. Continue building up the layers as described for the smaller inside flower.
3. When you have completed the 2nd layer of wool on both sides, place small amount of contrasting colour on the top of the template, as below (left).
4. Cover with netting, and flip to the other side, and bring the surplus wool over, as below (centre).
5. Repeat with a contrasting colour for the lower edge in the same way, as below (right).   
6. Continue felting as described for the smaller inside flower, following steps 11 to 15.
7. When the felt has shrunk, cut open, and remove the template.
8. Once the template has been removed, you are ready to commence the next stage.

Double Flower Form Method

Final Stage 
1. Make a small cut in the top of the larger flower, and thread the stem of the smaller flower through.
2. Sandwich the flower between 2 pieces of veggie netting, and sprinkle generously with hot soapy water, and rub a little extra soap on the surface on both sides. 
3. Press, and rub with your hands to stabilise the surface. Remove the net.
4. Place the flower on the ridged mat (or cane blind), and rub the base of the stem/top of the flower on the mat with your fingers, as below (left).
5. Commence rubbing the rest of the flower in the same manner (see below right) opening it out occasionally to ensure that the two sections of the flower are separated, i.e. the inside and outside.  
6. Open up the flower, and rub each section separately on the mat.  
7. Place the flower in a bowl, and pour boiling water over it to 'shock' it.
8. Rub the flower on a washboard, changing directions occasionally as you do so.
9. Rinse in warm water until all the soap has been removed.
10. Place in a Vinegar Rinse.
11. Spin dry, or towel dry.

Double Flower Form Method

You will notice that the flower sections have shrunk considerably from the sizes of the original templates.

Shaping and Finishing
1. Iron the flower with a hot iron until smooth. See below left.
2. Cut into the larger outer flower with a sharp pair of scissors. See below centre.
3. Iron each cut section smooth. See below right.

4. Cut the petals into the desired shapes. (Below left)
5. Iron smooth the inner flower section, and cut the petals as you did for the large flower section. Cut these into the desired shapes.
6. Iron the petals again, and while they are warm, shape them by pulling with your fingers to obtain a more sculptural appearance. (Below right)

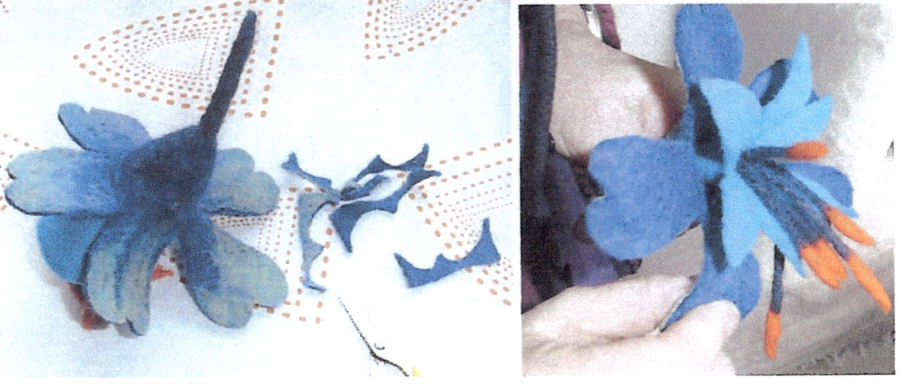

Assembly and Finishing
1. Cover florist wire by felting wool on to it, as previously described.
2. Twist the wires around the stem. (Below left)
3. Attach to the comb by twisting coloured wire over them to hold in place tightly. Cut the ends of the wire with a pair of wire cutters. (Below right)

Double Flower Form Method

When worn in your hair it can be that special finishing touch to your whole appearance!

'Orchid Cascade' headwear and decorative belt.

Headwear as Sculpture

Advanced Felted Wire Method

It is possible to combine several felting methods in order to produce an intricate 3-dimensional structure, which actually starts off flat but with the aid of embedded felted wires, the Form can be raised, when everything has felted together.

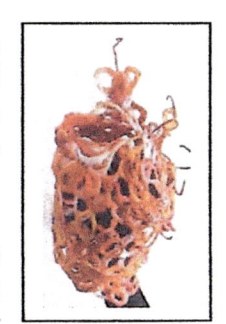

This type of work is certainly not for the absolute beginner, as it is quite complex, but once you realise the possibilities, you can adapt it to suit your needs.

Method

1. Prepare your work area, by placing a towel on the table to soak up any surplus water. Place the cane blind on top, and cover with a plastic sheet. Have ready a bowl of warm soapy water and a bar of glycerine soap.
2. Cut off lengths of millinery wire, and felt Merino wool on to them, but do not felt them too firmly. Leave them slightly under-felted. 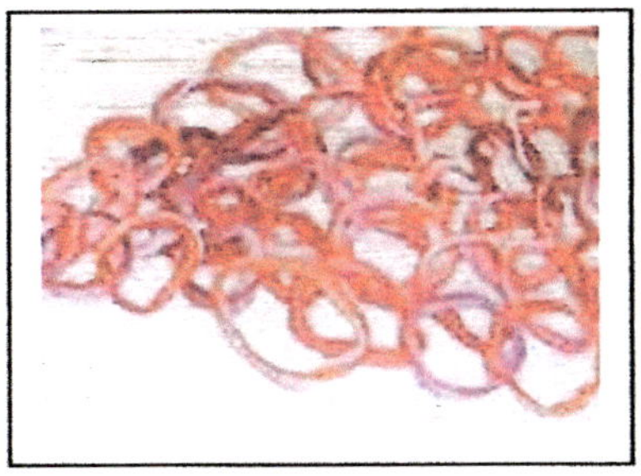
3. Place the felted wires to one side, while you build up the desired shape using the 'bubble felt' technique. This will form your 1st layer.
4. When you have completed this layer, place the felted wires in position.
5. Cover the whole area with the second layer of 'bubble' rings.
6. Take a piece of bubble-wrap, and soap it well.  
7. Turn the bubble-wrap over (bubble side down), and massage over the area to be felted.  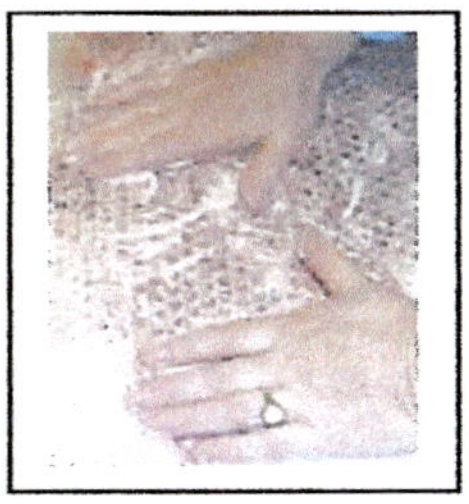
8. Continue massaging, until you see that the wool is beginning to hold together. Remove the towel that is under the cane blind. Remove the bubble-wrap, and cover with the other end of the cane blind. Pick up the whole lot and flip it over to the other side, and remove the plastic sheet that was in the blind. 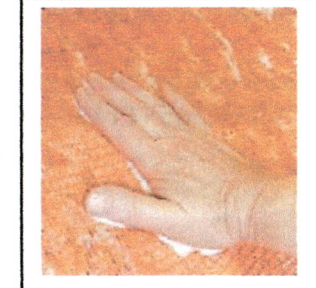
9. Repeat massaging with the soaped bubble-wrap in the same way as you worked the other side. Cover with the cane blind, and flip back to the first side.
10. Open the blind, and cover the work with a veggie net, and begin to rub vigorously with the flat of your

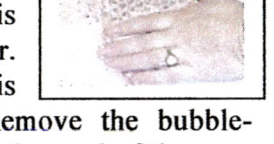

Headwear as Sculpture

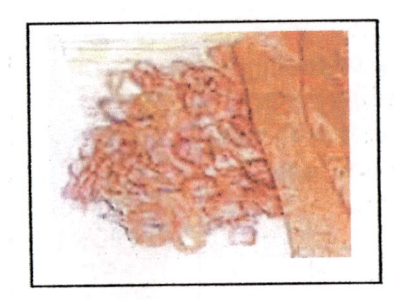

     hand, like a flatbed 'sander', working all over the entire surface.
11. Cover with the cane blind and flip the work over to the other side, and repeat. By now you should see that everything is beginning to stabilise, and hold together.
12. Begin to rub with your hands, massaging as you go. Turn the work over using the cane blind to support your piece, and rub that side with your hands. 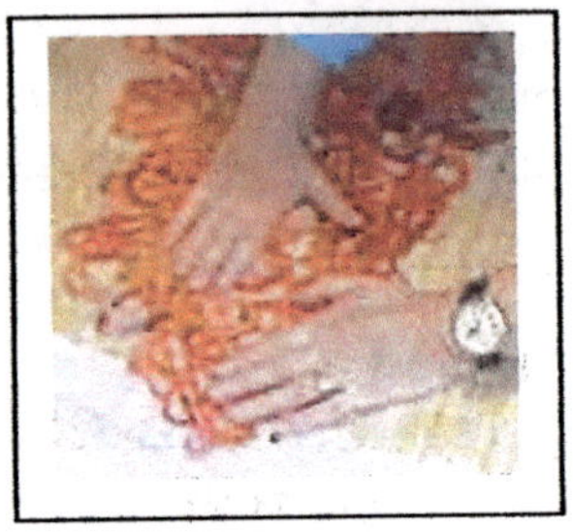 
13. Continue in this way, working with your hands on both sides, until everything holds together firmly, and there is not risk of anything falling apart, or moving.
14. You are now ready to pick up the whole piece, and rub it just in your hands, without the support of the blind. 
15. As soon as the entire piece has felted firmly together, you can rinse out the soap, and pass it through a vinegar rinse. Mop up the surplus water with a dry towel.
16. Shape the piece on a hat block, holding it in position with pins.
17. Leave to dry, and add any additional embellishments, such as beads, etc., by sewing them on.

That's it! Ta-da!

I am sure you will find many other ways of incorporating felted wire in between your layers in order to create 3-dimensional forms from a 2-dimensional beginning.

It may be awkward, and rather time-consuming, but in the end you will have the satisfaction of having overcome tremendous obstacles. What a great achievement!

Felted Mesh Method

In order to incorporate wire meshes into the layers of felt, it is necessary to use a different method for felt making to that described in the previously, because you cannot roll mesh or wire without the danger of breaking it. The technique to use is essentially a 'rubbing' method, which is usually worked flat as that is the easiest way, and then on completion, manipulated into the desired form. As in the previous chapter, this method of working allows you to make lightweight, yet firm self-supporting sculptural forms – large or small.

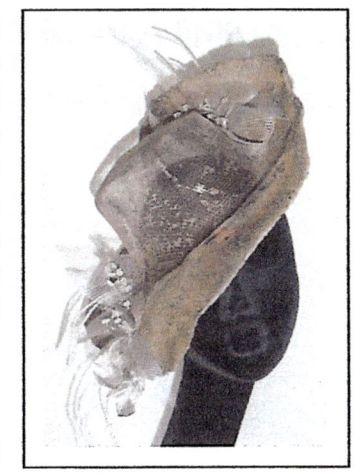

What you need
- ✓ Cane blind on ridged mat, placed on old towel on the table
- ✓ Glycerine soap and Sprinkle bottle with soap solution
- ✓ 2 x pieces of Bubble Wrap
- ✓ Piece of veggie sacking
- ✓ Merino 64's Wool 'Tops'
- ✓ Metal mesh, or chicken wire that has been cut into shape, and the edges turned over with a pair of pliers
- ✓ Pair of heavy-duty rubber gloves to protect your hands
- ✓ A felting tool, e.g. a block of wood with grooves cut into it, or a massage aid that will allow you to rub the surface without having to place your hands directly on a surface where wire ends may be protruding, which could cut you
- ✓ Hand towel
- ✓ Vinegar rinse, as for flat basic felts

What you do
1. Place a towel on the table, and put a cane blind on top, or ridged mat. Place a piece of bubble wrap on top. Place the wire mesh on to the plastic, and cover with a thin layer of Merino wool (Side 'A'). Sprinkle with soap solution. Cover with the second 'bubble' sheet, and pick up this 'sandwich', and flip it over on to the other side.
2. Remove the top plastic sheet, and bring the surplus ends of the wool over the edges on to side 'B'. Cover side 'B' with a thin layer of wool. Sprinkle with soap solution, cover with 'bubble' sheet, and turn back over to side 'A'. Bring the surplus wool over the edge on to side 'A'. Cover with plastic, and turn back over to side 'B'.
3. Remove top 'bubble' sheet, and soap generously with bar of glycerine soap. Begin to massage gently the surface with the soapy bubble wrap.

Felted Mesh Method

4. Replace the plastic, and turn over to the other side (side 'A'), and repeat stage 3.
5. Continue massaging with the bubble wrap, alternately on both sides until the surface begins to stabilise (a). Increase the pressure and rub more vigorously as the fibres begin to 'knit' together (b).

(a) 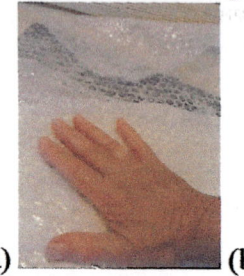　　(b)

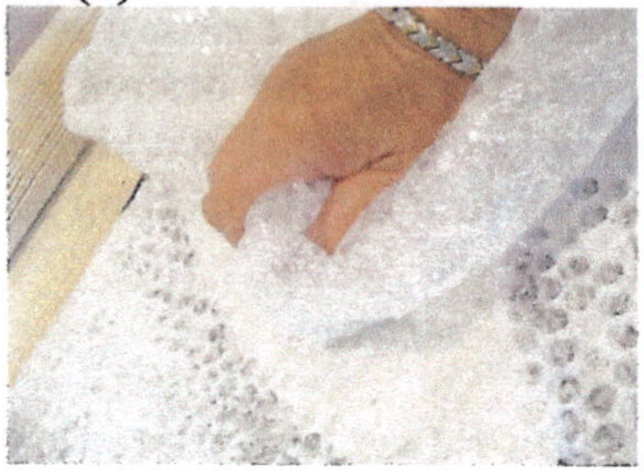

6. Remove the bubble wrap when the fibres are beginning to hold more firmly together.

(fig. A)

7. Cover with the veggie sacking, and begin to rub the surface, using it like a sander. Repeat this on both sides, increasing the pressure as you proceed. Wrap the veggie sacking round a block of wood to help protect your hands, when you do this.
8. Continue rubbing the surfaces in this manner until the fibres stop moving completely. 
9. If you have a felting tool (See fig. A, above) or massager, begin to rub the surfaces without any netting. 

Alternately, rub carefully with your hands so as not to cut yourself on any exposed wire ends.

Felted Mesh Method

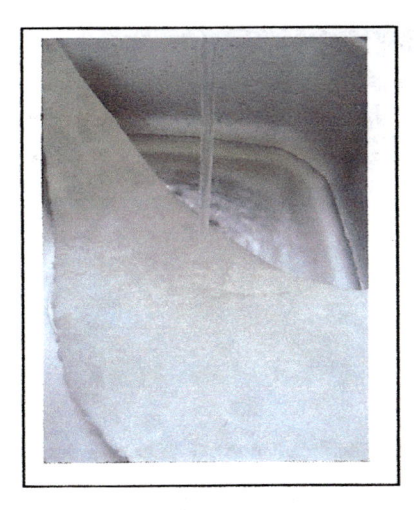

10. By now the fibres should be firmly entangled together, and have formed a firm bonding with the wire mesh. Rinse in warm water until the water runs clear.
11. Pass through a Vinegar rinse as described before, and remove excess moisture with a dry towel.
12. Manipulate the felted mesh into the form that you require, and leave to dry.

It is now ready to be treated with stiffeners and other surface treatments.

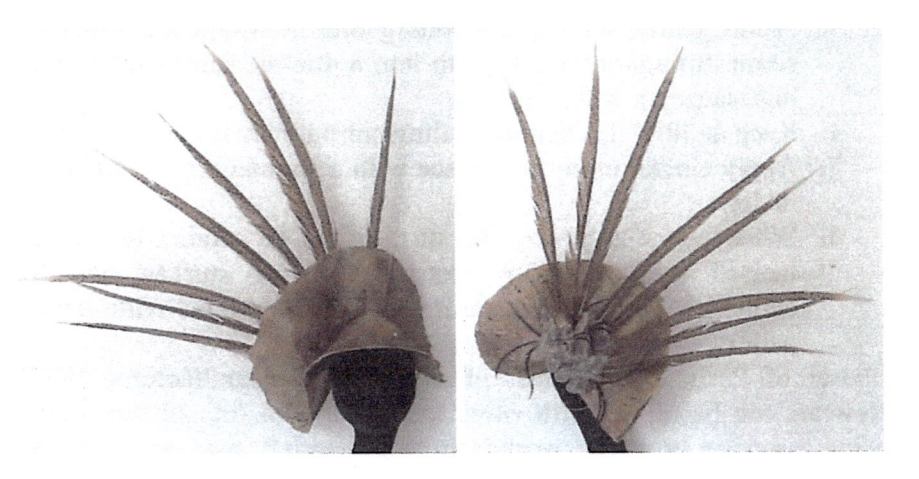

While the mesh felt is still damp, it will absorb stiffeners most easily.

Stiffeners you can use

- ❖ PVA diluted with water to a consistency of 50 : 50 ratio (c), and applied to the surface with a sponge brush (d).

Felted Mesh Method

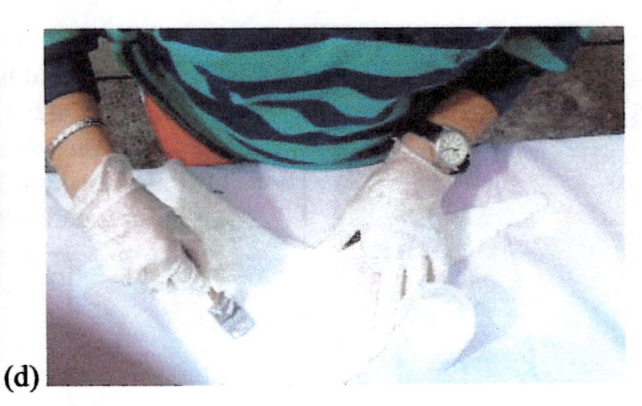

(c)   (d)

- ❖ Gesso is a medium, which when mixed with an adhesive and applied to a surface, hardens to such an extent that it resembles stone, or ceramics. When completely dry, it can then be sanded and carved, and treated like any stone-like substance.
    1. Dissolve 28 g Rabbit Skin Glue in 426 ml of water.
    2. Mix 3 parts weight of Gesso powder with 4 parts weight of glue solution in old saucepan. **Add powder to the glue solution, and not solution to powder, otherwise you will get lumps!**
    3. Warm gently, stirring continually until thoroughly combined. If lumpy, strain through a muslin cloth into a double saucepan (or old bowl, set in a saucepan with water).
    4. Keep at 40°C for ½ hour to allow air bubbles to rise, and stir gently.
    5. Apply Gesso on to the surface with a sponge brush, quickly, and leave to dry.
    6. When completely dry, the surface can be sanded to be smooth, and incised with a sharp instrument. The surface can be further embellished, if desired, or drawn into, or painted with acrylics and oil paints.
- ❖ Plaster of Paris, or 'Wallart' plastic medium manufactured by Winsor & Newton, can be mixed with water and applied to the surface of a mesh felt, using a sponge brush, or worked in with hands*, and once that has dried, it will be as hard as rock. Once it has set, you can sand it, paint it, spray it, etc. to your heart's content! If you find that colour sinks into the surface, size the surface first with PVA.
- ❖ 'Paverpol' is another stiffening agent that can be used. It looks very like PVA, and is applied in the same way, but unlike PVA, it retains the appearance of felt, without the plastic-like finish.

* Make sure you are wearing rubber gloves to protect your hands.
Remember always to add powder to water, stirring continually.

Gallery

Once you have mastered the various felting and millinery techniques, you will be amazed at the diversity of ideas you can translate into headwear. There are no limits to what you can do.

Over the years I have made some extraordinary creations; each one has forced myself to explore new possibilities. These challenges have propelled me forward – thus extending my knowledge and expertise. Furthermore, teaching situations present me with challenges as students' ideas and designs, demand me to help them achieve the realisation of their notions in a finished hat of a satisfactory standard. I am continually surprised at what is possible, and I would urge you to be adventurous, and challenge yourself with constant problem-solving situations, so that you too can discover your true potential.

Therefore in this section, I would like to share with you work by my students and me, that challenge convention and open up opportunities for pure creativity, and for overcoming the seemingly 'impossible'.

Photo: Mica's hat incorporating metal mesh that had been burnt out. The idea for the hat came from an illustration of an abandoned, rusty ship.

When I first began making hats, I had to improvise my hat 'blocks', and therefore I resorted to using a flowerpot!

A commission for a show-stopping hat for a Chair-lady of a Flower Society, led me to making the 'Sweet pea Basket' hat - a tremendous challenge at the time, but terrific fun! I do not know if she ever had the courage to wear it, but I certainly learned a lot making it.

Gallery

A Selection of Students' hats from workshops at Alston Hall, Lancashire, and Missenden Abbey, Buckinghamshire

a) Hat by Gillian Hill, Alston Hall
b) Hat by Jenny Jones, Alston Hall
c) And d) 'Dragon' hat for her son, by Mica Trace-Kleeberg, Missenden Abbey
e) Hat by Melanie Bermingham, Missenden Abbey
f) A variation on a beret by Susan Byrne, Alston Hall

Technical Tips

'Pre-felts' for well defined shapes

Preparation:
Either tease out randomly dyed wool, and lay two thin layers of wool, each at 90° to the other on a piece of nylon net, or place fine handfuls of variously toned colours, as illustrated.

Method: 
1. Cover with another piece of nylon netting, and sprinkle with warm soapy water. Rub extra soap on the bubble wrap and massage on both sides of the layers.
2. Commence rolling, quarter-turning as you go until you reach the stage when you remove the netting, i.e. when you have completed rolling on both sides.
3. Remove the netting, and **stop!** Do not roll any more. 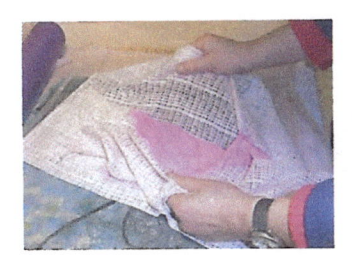
4. If the wool is very wet, dab it with a dry towel before you try to pick it up.

It is now ready for use, and you can cut out the motifs for your project.

'Pointillist' Effect

You can pull off and lay down small amounts of wool from your 'Tops' with your fingers to represent streaks of paint made by a brush. If you wish to create a dappled effect like the Pointillist painter, Seurat, pull off lengths of wool in mixed colours. Hold them firmly and cut off tiny snippets from the ends.

Felt Stiffener

There are occasions when it is necessary to apply a stiffener to the finished felt hat, e.g. when you have a wide-brimmed hat made in fine felt. Without it, the brim would flop. I have found that ***Crodacoat Stiffener M6224*** is very effective. It is however, highly flammable and should only be used in well-ventilated conditions. Nevertheless it is easy to apply with a 2" brush (household painting type) on the inside of the hat. **It is important to protect the felt from any moisture, as water affects the stiffener and turns it white.** When applying the stiffener, do so evenly, and leave to dry completely before applying the next coat. Continue in this way until about 4 coats have been applied. Try and avoid allowing the stiffener to seep through on to the right side of the hat, as this may mark the surface. When used

Technical Tips

correctly, the stiffener dries out transparent. Brushes should be cleaned after each use with 'Acetone', which is also flammable and should not be inhaled. It is therefore essential that the cleaning of brushes should be done in well-ventilated conditions.

Is there a cheap and effective felt stiffener that is easy to obtain?
Try using 'Extra Firm Hold' Hair Spray. This is readily available in your local shops, and is extremely effective. I use it in preference to commercial hat stiffeners, especially as now it is difficult to obtain the spirit-based variety. It is perfect for firming up cut and curled pieces. (See p.17) What is more, the hair spray does not seem to be affected by rain, and it does not discolour the surface.

Painterly Effects for Hats

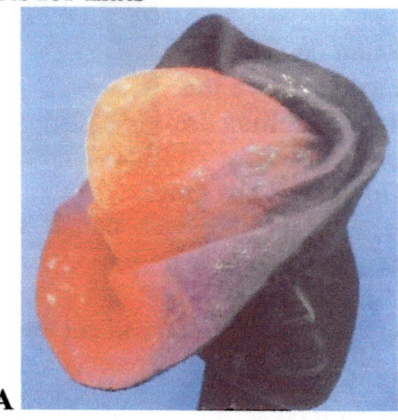

A   B

Example A
The hat illustrates not only the painterly application of colours in the build up of the layers, but also the incorporation of metallic net fragments. As the idea behind this hat, was to depict a volcano and molten lava, I added these tiny pieces of glitz to evoke the sparkle of fire and flames.

Example B
In this depiction of a 'Tsunami' wave, not only did I 'paint' with the fibres and incorporate fragments of shiny fabric, to evoke its watery colouring and sparkle, but also I invented a new way of working with fibres. I wanted to create an impression of foam, and in order to do this I pulled off small lengths of dyed 'Tops' and wound them around my fingers to form hollow circles, like sliced onion rings, or 'Polo' mints. I proceeded to lay these down in overlapping rows around the brim edge and at the top of the hat's crown. My intention was to create open lace-like effects like bubbles, rather than just painting into the normal solid layers for felt hats. Once the hat was complete, I added further details to enhance the 'frothiness' of the foam on the crown, by sewing iridescent sequins, glass and pearl beads.

Brims
Edges of brims can be distressed by brushing with a teasel brush. (See right) This creates a soft edge

When shaping brims, during 'blocking', they can be flattened out by pounding with a 'meat tenderiser' or mallet, and steamed while damp with a hot iron. As you press with the

Technical Tips

iron, support the inside and outside alternately with a towel.

Substitutes for Ridged Plastic Mats

In this book, I have used ridged plastic place mats, which I bought from IKEA, but I realise that they may not be readily available. Therefore look out for suitable substitutes, e.g. rubber car mats, non-slip shower mats, etc. I have found them extremely useful for a wide range of felting situations.

Attaching 'Brim Reed' or Millinery Wire

There are occasions when it is necessary to attach either 'brim reed' or millinery wire to the edge of a brim. This is especially necessary when the felt is very fine and lace-like, or when you it is needed to support an intricate brim shape.

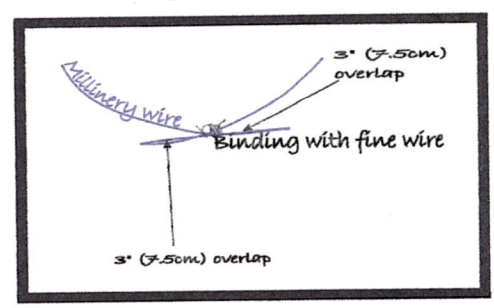

1. Calculate the circumference of the brim, and add a further 6" (15cm), which will allow for the overlap and adjustments.
2. Overlap the ends of the wire, and bind them together at a point 3" (7.5cm) from the end. Use either fine silver wire, or a triangular piece of 'sellotape' for the binding.
3. Hold the wire in position approximately ½" (1cm) in from the edge of the brim, and fix with pins at regular intervals all the way round. It is easier to keep the tension evenly distributed, by starting the pinning at opposite sides to each other, e.g. front and back, side A to side B, and then at points ½ way between these, until the whole wire has been secured in place with pins.
4. Oversew the wire in position, making sure that you keep your stitching invisible on the outside of the felt, as seen in diagram 'A' on right.
5. Bring the edge of the felt over the wire, and stitch into place with a 'ladder stitch', making sure that you keep your stitching small and neat. (Diagram 'A') As you fold the felt over the wire, you may find that you need to trim it so that it just covers the wire, and no more.
6. Roll the covering felt with your fingers, over the wire to ensure that not wire is showing. (Diagram 'B')

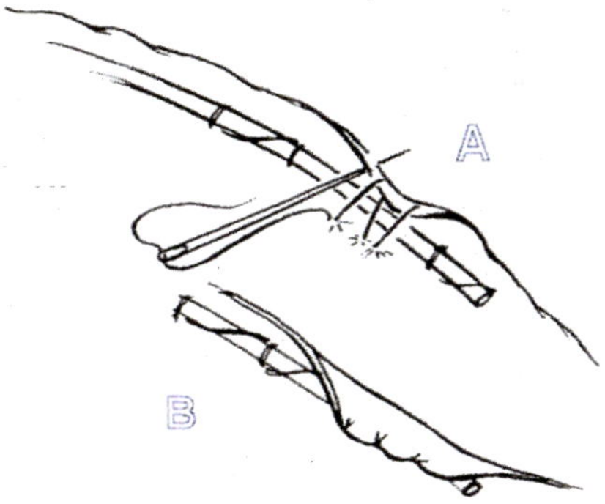

Finishing Touch – Attaching the 'Petersham' ribbon on the inside

In most handmade felt hats this is not necessary, but occasionally it is required. It is an especially effective way for adjusting the size of a hat to fit a client. Traditionally, it is used to disguise the join of the brim to the crown, but in handmade hats this is not necessary, as the brim and crown are 'all-in-one'.

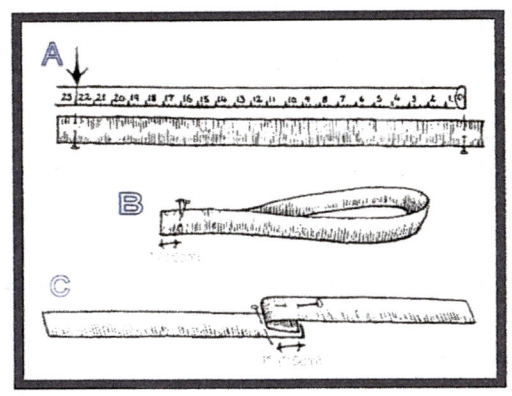

(A) Measure the head size, and add 1" (2.5cm) for comfort. Place a pin 1" from the end of the ribbon, and start

Technical Tips

    the measurement from this point. Place a pin at the required length, and add 1" (2.5cm) before cutting at this point.
(B) Bring the ends together at this point, leaving the 1" (2.5cm) overlap.
(C) Fold one end over, as illustrated, and pin together. Stitch neatly together along this folded edge.

Turn the ribbon over and trim one end of the ribbon with a diagonal cut to about ½ cm of the stitched join. Fold the other end over this to cover it, and fold the raw edge over. Sew neatly into place.

Never cut the ends of the ribbon too close, otherwise there will be no room left for further adjustments should they be needed.

Pin the join of the 'Petersham' ribbon to the inside of the hat at the back, and at the halfway point, pin to the front of the hat. Pin the ribbon to the hat at the side, half way between front and back; and repeat on the opposite side. Continue pinning the ribbon in this manner, midway between the pins, until the pins are approximately 1" (2.5cm) apart.

Sew neatly in place, easing the felt as you progress, so that it does not pucker. Make sure that no stitches show on the outside of the hat. If they do, you can disguise these by placing a decorative felt cord, or ribbon, over the top.

In Conclusion

I have endeavoured to present to you a number of different methods for making a diversity of hats and headwear – some simple; some complex – in the hope that it will encourage you to try these techniques out for yourself, and give you the confidence to undertake greater challenges in the process.

It is impossible to cover every aspect thoroughly enough within the limitations of the number of pages that this book allows. More pages would make the resulting book, more expensive, and therefore I have curtailed myself by covering as thoroughly as I can the essential techniques that are required for the various types of projects in the category of 'Hats and Headwear'. In order to present the material as a 'whole', I have included topics covered in my previous books. These I have updated, to keep the information as current as possible.

I do so in the hope that you will find that having all the information between one set of covers, a useful source of reference, and that you will have a go and strive towards producing imaginative quality results.

Remember, everything is possible, because there is always a solution to a design problem – and if your felt does not allow you to reflect your original idea exactly; then follow the direction dictated by the felt you have made, and save that first notion for another day. Every time you set out to make your felt hat, even though you may use the same template, it will turn out differently, because each day we approach our work differently. The way we handle the materials will differ, as will the actual working methods.

        It is an adventure – enjoy the ride!

Glossary

Some of the words I have used throughout the book may not be familiar to you, so to help you understand what I mean, I have included a list that you may find useful. I must add that they are not necessarily those found in dictionaries. They are explained in MY terms to convey MY meaning.

Alice band	Also known as 'hair band' and 'head band'.
Blocking	Forming a finished felt on a mould, e.g. hat block, shoe last, etc.
Brim Reed	Clear plastic filament, available in different thicknesses, ideal to use on lightweight and lacy hats
Clingfilm	Also known as 'surround-wrap' (USA).
Fulling	Shrinking the felt to make it more compressed and denser.
Merino	Type of sheep, raised in Australia and New Zealand for its fineness.
Millinery Wire	A thread covered wire used traditionally in millinery. Can be obtained in different thicknesses.
Petersham	A 'grossgrain' ribbon, which is firm and non-stretchy
Pilling	The tendency for the woollen surface to roll itself into tiny balls.
Tops	Commercially prepared combed wool, ready for spinning.
64's	These refer to 'wool counts', determining the quality of the wool fibre.

- The lower the number; the coarser the wool. Thus 64's wool is finer than 50's.

Illustrations

Throughout this book, all diagrams and photographs have been prepared by the author, unless stated otherwise. Occasionally Sandy McDonald has taken photographs when my hands have been occupied.

Front Cover
Anemone digital images; 'Sea Anemone' hat.

Introduction
p.1: Miner's felt hat, Geevor Mining Museum, Cornwall

Chapter 1 : Preparation
p.3: 4 images of workshop area and equipment; 1 hat block and 'meat tenderiser'
p.4: Turned hat blocks; vegetable net; 2 images of Merino 'Tops'

Chapter 2 : Exploring a Theme
p.5: 6 images of corals and sea-life, taken at the Sea Life Centre, North Queensferry
p.5: 2 images of books and reference material
p.6: fish bag; 11 Hat inspired by sea-life; 2 images of Head Wear

Chapter 3 : Seamless Felting Method
p.7: 3 diagrams for making preparations for a 'Resist' template
p.8: diagram for making 'Resist' variations; Images of 'Cacti' hats, 'Hoopoe' hat; 'Hunderwasser' hat
p.9: 6 images of Hat Blocks; Image of Wooden Hat Stretcher
p.10: Image of the preparation of the work area
p.11: 4 images of stages of seamless felting
p.12: 5 images of stages of seamless felting
p.15: 3 images of blocking hat; image of finished 'Angelfish' hat; image of Missenden Abbey Hat Workshop class
p.16: 3 images of hats changed through dyeing; 3 images of 'Monet' hat; image of 'Seurat' hat; image of restyled 'Seurat' hat
p.17: 7 images of various 'Spiral' hats; diagram of Cloche template; images of 'Klimt' hat, 'Bug' hat, 'Santa Monica' hat
p.18: Image of 'Liquorice Allsorts' hat; diagram of 'Bell' template; image of 'Feather' hat, 'Hundertwasser' hat; hat by Ewina Wilkes; diagram of extended bell template; images of 'Patisserie' hats, remodelled hat 'A', remodelled hat 'B

Chapter 4: Multi-form Seamless Felting Method
p.19: Image of 'Sea Urchin' hat; 3 images of stages in the preparation of multiform seamless technique
p.20: 8 images of stages in multi-form seamless method
p.21: 7 images of stages in multi-form seamless method
p.22: Image of multi-form seamless stage; 3 images of 'blocking' and shaping hat; 2 images of 'Sea Swirl' hat

Chapter 5: Berets
p.23: Image of 'Pizza' beret, 'Strawberry' beret and accessories, 'Holly' beret and accessories, 'Ladybird' beret; diagram of opening variations; diagram of developing basics
p.24: 2 images of beret with fabric inserts and surface embroidery

Illustrations

p.24: 3 images of beret by Claudie Tingley (Photos: Artur Tingley)
p.25: 4 diagrams of circular beret variations; image of shell fragment
p.26: 4 images of felting method for complex berets
p.27: 3 images of finishing and ironing complex beret; 3 views of completed 'Shell' beret

Chapter 6 : Mixed Media Fascinators
p.29: 3 images of various mixed media fascinators; image of equipment and materials; image of 1st stage of preparation for felting wire
p.30: 3 images of felting wire; image of finished shaped wires
p.31: 2 images of assembling fascinator; image of attaching fascinator on to comb; image of finished fascinator
p.32: 2 images of fascinators attached to hair bands; image of 'Orchid' Fascinator, 'Titania's Crown', 'Swarming Butterflies' Headwear and necklace

Chapter 7 : Felt Flower Head Pieces
p.33: Images of selection of completed flowers; group of flowers on hair slide; small rollers and flower; flower templates in various sizes; 1st stage of felting stamen
p.34: Image of completed stamen; attaching stem to stamen; 2 images of felting stem
p.35: 9 images of stages of making flower
p.36: Images of complete flower; flower and covered head band; 2 images of wrapped and felted hair band; complete assembly of flower on felted head band; assorted flowers; 'Lily hat; 'Bird with Lilies' head band

Chapter 8 : Double Flower Form Method
p.37: Image of double flower on comb; 4 images of stages in double flower method
p.38: 7 images of stages of double flower felting
p.39: 7 images of double flower felting stages
p.40: 6 images of double flower felting stages
p.41: Image of felted flower compared to original templates; 5 images of shaping and finishing flower; attaching felted wires to stem; attaching to comb
p.42: Image of completed double flower fascinator; fascinator being worn by Ewa; 'Orchid Cascade' Headwear and decorative belt

Chapter 9 : Headwear as Sculpture – Advanced Felted Wire Method
p.43: 2 images of 'Coral Reef' headwear; 4 images of stages in preparation of felting method
p.44: 3 images of felting stages; completed headwear, drying on hat block; finished 'Coral Reef'

Chapter 10 : Felted Mesh Method
p.45: Image of 'Metallo' hat; 2 images of stages in felting method
p.46: 7 images of stages of felting technique
p.47: 2 images of finishing stages of mesh method; 2 images of 'Fan-cosmic' hat; various stiffeners that can be used
p.48: 2 images of PVA solution and application to mesh felt

Chapter 11 : Gallery
p.49: Image of Ewa with Mica Trace-Kleeberg; 2 images of 'Oops' hat; 2 images of 'Sweet pea Basket' hat

Illustrations

p.50: Image of hat by Gillian Hill; hat by Jenny Jones; 2 images of 'Dragon' hat by Mica Trace-Kleeberg; hat by Melanie Bermingham; beret by Susan Byrne

Chapter 12 : Technical Tips
p.51: 3 images of making 'Pre-felts'; 3 images for creating 'Pointillist' surface effect; 'Crodacoat' felt stiffener
p.52: Image of 'Volcano' hat; 'Tsunami' hat; hat with softened edges by a member of the Cornish Felting Group
p.53: Diagrams – binding millinery wire together; sewing millinery wire in place; preparation of 'petersham' ribbon (based on drawings by Denise Innes)

About the Author
p.65: Photo by James Hensby

Resources

U.K. Suppliers

- **All types of wool 'tops' and fibres, fancy yarns, felting tools, equipment:**

Wingham Woolwork
70 Main Street
Wentworth
Rotherham
S. Yorkshire
S62 7BR   tel. 01226-742926   fax: 01226-741166
Website: http://www.wingwool.clara.net

- **Custom made Hat blocks**

Guy Morse-Brown
Mill Lane Farmhouse
Mill Lane
Wombourne
WV5 0LE   tel. 01902-893683   Website: http://www.hatblocks.co.uk

- **Dyes for wool and silk ('Omega'), and dyes for cotton, linen, etc (cold water 'Procion', and hot water 'Dyrect')**

Colourcraft Ltd
Unit 5
555 Carlisle Street East
Sheffield
S.Yorks.
S4 8DT   tel: 0114-2421431   Email: colourcraftltd@aol.com
Website: http://www.colourcraftltd.com

- **Metal Mesh, Wire, Paverpol**

The Smithfield Gallery
Lancaster
Tel: 01524-762883
Email: info@smithfieldgallery.co.uk Website: http://www.smithfieldgallery.co.uk

- **Millinery Supplies** (inc. Millinery wire and 'Brim Reed', stiffeners)

Baxter Hart & Abraham Ltd.
141 New Bedford Road,
Luton,
Beds.
LU3 1LF   tel: 01582-721381   fax: 01582-405726

- **'Paverpol', wide selection of Art and Craft Materials**

Art Van Go
1 Stevenage Road,
Knebworth,
Herts.
SG3 6AN   tel: 01438-814946
Email: art@artvango.co.uk   Website: http://www.artvango.co.uk

Resources

☐ **Stiffener for Felt**
Croda Paints Ltd
Saxon Works
Rutland Road
Sheffield, S3 9PU   tel: 0114 272 1264   fax: 0114 275 0503

U.S.A. Suppliers

☐ **Hat Blocks** (Wooden)
Jim Prichard, Windsor Hollow Farm, 205 Chase's Pond Road, York, Maine 03909
tel: 1-207-363-8163   E-mail: felting@nh.ultranet.com

☐ **Hat Blocks** (Polystyrene)
Franks Cane & Rush Supply, 7252 Heil Avenue, Huntington Beach, CA 92647
Tel. 714 – 847-0707   Fax: 714 – 843-5645

☐ **Merino Wool 'Tops'**
Ashland Bay Trading Co., PO Box. 2613, Gig Harbor, WA 98335
Tel: 1-253-851-6150 or 1-800-213-0628

The Wool Shed, PO Box 153, Hewitt, TX 76643   tel: 1-254-666-0334
E-mail: woolshed@juno.com
Website: http://www.Outbackfibers.com

☐ **Millinery Supplies**
Alexander, Baum & Berlin, 707 South Broadway, 11th Floor, L.A., CA 90014
Tel: 213 – 622-7064 / 213 – 622-3388

California Millinery Supply, 721 South Spring Street, L.A., CA 90014
Tel: 213 – 622-8746   E-mail: calmil@loop.com

Hats by Leko, 2081 Buffalo Street, Caspar, WY 82604   E-mail: hatsupply@aol.com

Manny's Millinery, 26 West 38th Street, New York, NY 10018   Tel: 212 – 840-2235

Milliner's Supply Co., 911 Elm Street, Dallas, TX 75202   tel: 214 – 742-7284
Website: http://www.milliners.com

☐ **Yarns and Fibres**
Susan's Fiber Shop
N250 County Road A
Columbus, WI 53925   tel: 920-623-4237   E-mail: susanfiber@internetwis.com

Resources

Literature worth consulting

Art of the Feltmaker Mary Burkett, published by Abbot Hall Art Gallery ISBN 0 9503335 1 4

Classic Millinery Techniques Ann Albrizio, Oznat, 1999; available from Amazon.co.uk

Echoes Quarterly journal by International Feltmakers Association

Dyeing to Colour Bailey Curtis, 7 Lancaster Terrace, Hill Top Lane, Newent, Glos., GL18 1EA ISBN 0-9541419-0-3

Fabulous Felt Hats Chad Alice Hagen, 2005, published by Lark Books ISBN 1-57990-542-0 (hardcover)

Filz Felt Ed. Katharina Thomas, published by Arnoldsche Art Publishers

Hats made Easy (Milner Craft Series) Lyn Waring, published by Sally Milner Pub. Pty. Ltd., 2004

Hats on Heads Mildred Anlezark, published by Kangaroo Press, 1992 ISBN 0 86417 303 2

New Directions for Felt Gunilla Paetau Sjöberg, English translation published by Interweave Press ISBN 1-883010-17-9

North American Felters' Newsletter Patricia Spark, 1032 SW Washington St., Albany, Oregon 97321 USA

The Hat Book Juliet Bawden, published by Charles Letts, 1992 ISBN 1-85238-332-1

The Hat Magazine ed. Carole Denford, The Hat Magazine Ltd., 170 Brick Lane, London, E1 6RU Website: http://www.thehatmagazine.com

The Mummies of Ürümchi Elizabeth Wayland Barber, published Macmillan ISBN 0 333 73024 0

Websites worth visiting

Ewa Kuniczak: http://www.feltheadtotoe.co.uk

Useful Contacts for Feltmakers

- International Feltmakers Association : Website:http://www.feltmakers.org.uk
- Scottish Felters: Website: http://felthtt.dircon.co.uk/scottishfelters.htm
- North American Felters' Network: Website:http://www.peak.org/~spark/feltmakers.html

Resources

Future Publications

"Felting Rainbows": Creative Dyeing for Felters – planned for August 2005
Exciting ways to create painterly and pattern effects into wool prior to felting, as well as fully illustrated explanations of a wide range of 'resist' techniques after felting animal and plant fibres and cloth. A must for all who would like to add a very personal colour dimension to their work.

"Words to Fibre Books" – planned for Spring 2006
I have a life-long enjoyment of reading and the actual process of turning pages over as the 'story' unfolds. Books have always held a fascination for me, and here I intend to examine different ways of contrasting fibre books where felts and fibre papers are combined with various surface treatments and stitchery, together with painting and printing to make very personal 'Art Books', that do not necessarily conform to the usual rectangular format. Books and Book Boxes are given as much consideration as their content, and as for the reasons for making them.

"Sculpting and Painting with Needles": Developments with Dry Felting Techniques – planned for Summer 2007
The aim of this book is to demonstrate the potential of dry needle felting methods beyond that which were covered in 'Felt Figures Great and Small'. My travels have brought me in contact with many gifted fibre artists, and my own recent work has been exploring new possibilities and projects which I hope will encourage you to discover more ways of working in isolation, or in combination with other felting methods. Furthermore, I intend to examine creatively the use of needling machines, which are currently available in the market-place, and which can be used to add colour, texture, and detail to surfaces, as well as other useful purposes.

About the Author

An Honours graduate in Art Education with a Postgraduate Diploma in Textile Art, Ewa taught Art and Design from 1969 until she decided to devote her time to her own work, and went completely freelance in 1987. Whenever possible, she teaches in Schools, Colleges, and leads Community Projects. She has also undertaken felting projects with Special Needs groups, working with disadvantaged young adults, adults, some of whom are blind. For several weeks every year, she and Sandy travel overseas, where she runs workshops. She has taught at Arrowmont School of Art and Crafts, in Tennessee, and at the Michigan Fiber Festival, as well as many places in Southern California, Wisconsin, New York State, Texas, and New Hampshire. In 2004, she taught at the Summer Academy in Bremanger, Norway, and in Eire. In 2005 she and Sandy are heading off to Australia and New Zealand to teach and have fun. Never at a stand still!

In 1995, Ewa set up her business, 'Felt Head to Toe', specialising in handmade seamless felt items for Adults, Children and the Home. She continues to supply Galleries and Retail outlets throughout the U.K., and exports primarily to Japan and U.S.A., as well as selling directly at prestigious Craft Fairs, undertaking private commissions, and regularly exhibiting in the U.K. and abroad. Her work has been featured in many magazines, newspapers and books, as well as T.V.

She lives and works in Kincardine-on-Forth, Fife, and enjoys working on her computer, where she designs and prints all her books and promotional material. For several years she has embraced e-commerce via her website which she set up and maintains herself, http://www.feltheadtotoe.co.uk , and in 2003 launched http://www.feltheadtotoe.com , her Online Shopping site. She lists 'working on her computer' as one of her hobbies.

Her Family is a constant joy to her, and she takes great pride in their achievements. Her son, Ian and his family, and her daughter, Lynn and her family, have always made Life even more meaningful and worthwhile.

For the last fourteen years, Sandy has been her constant companion, home organiser, mentor, business partner, exhibition 'roadie', and fellow traveller. He is her best friend, and without his support, sense of humour and patience, there would be no 'felt in the kitchen', or anywhere else in, or outside, the house! She is very indebted to him for his continued loyal and loving support, and in 2002 she become his wife and a member of the McDonald clan.

Photo credit: James Hensby, 2005